CAKE
STYLE

The Art of Cake Decorating

CAKE
STYLE

The Art of Cake Decorating

ANNIE DAM

Search Press

This edition published in 2011 by
Search Press Ltd
Wellwood
North Farm Road
Tunbridge Wells
Kent TN2 3DR
www.searchpress.com

A Quintet book
Copyright © Quintet Publishing Limited
All rights reserved.
QTT.CCHI

ISBN: 978-1-84448-780-6

This book was conceived, designed and produced by
Quintet Publishing Limited,
The Old Brewery,
6 Blundell Street,
London N7 9BH, UK

Project Editor: Holly Willsher
Copyeditor: Cary Hull
Designers: The Urban Ant
Photographer: Maki Blazevski
Art Director: Michael Charles
Managing Editor: Donna Gregory
Publisher: Mark Searle

Printed by 1010 Printing International Ltd, China

10 9 8 7 6 5 4 3 2 1

CONTENTS

INTRODUCTION 6

CAKE DECORATING MATERIALS... 8

CAKE DECORATING TOOLS........10

BASIC RECIPES 12

ESSENTIAL DECORATING

    TECHNIQUES 16

INDEX 142

VIOLET SCROLLS
22

CUBE
26

JAPANESE-
INSPIRED TEA CAKE
30

BLACK & WHITE
RIBBONS
34

RIBBON ROSES
40

COSMOPOLITAN
44

GIFT BOX
48

RUFFLED BROOCH
56

POLKA DOTS
62

MARDI GRAS
68

MOSAIC
76

BAROQUE
80

BABY SHOWER
86

TOPSY TURVY
94

FANCY CUSHION
100

ROSE BOUQUET
106

LUSTROUS PEACOCK
112

URBAN SAFARI
120

STREET SCENE
128

WEDDING DRESS
136

INTRODUCTION

I have always been fascinated by cake decorating and sugar-craft. It involves all forms of art, from sculpting to moulding to painting. And not only is it pretty to look at, it is great to eat. Just remember that inspiration can come from all places.

Living with my parents as new immigrants in Canada, there were never any Western desserts in the house. I decided that I needed to take matters into my own hands and started to collect recipes for cakes, biscuits and ice cream. I remember trying to make chocolate mousse one day when my parents were out and having to hide whipped cream, eggs and tins of melted chocolate when they came home unexpectedly. I didn't want them to discover my obsession with Western desserts.

During my years abroad in France and Spain, I had the opportunity to develop my real passion, combining art with my love for baking. As I perfected my style and learned new techniques, my cakes became more popular. I loved the feeling of everyone appreciating my art and thus my career as a cake decorator was born.

The concept behind *Cake Style* is to design beautiful edible art that makes everyone forget it is cake. The fact that our cakes become the centre of attention at so many special and important events in people's lives pushes us to provide the most amazing creations.

In the following pages, I will guide you step by step, teaching you how to create beautiful cakes for your own special events. As you work through each project in this book, from the simple to the elaborate, you will begin to gain the skills and experience to design your own creations. The innovative designs and handy tips and tricks will transform the baking beginner into a confectionery expert.

It's very easy to adapt these designs to fit your special occasion. Each project can be personalised by adding your own touch of creativity. You can change the colours and experiment with the different decorating techniques featured throughout the book to achieve a more personal design. Use the original projects as a launching pad and make something really wonderful for your loved ones. Just allow your imagination to run wild and enjoy yourself. Your cake can become a real work of edible art.

Have fun looking through all the projects and get ready to be inspired!

CAKE DECORATING MATERIALS

> To decorate a cake, such as the ones in this book, you will need specific materials – beginning with the cake itself.

Cakes, Buttercream Icing, & Royal Icing

You can make any flavour of cake you want for any of the designs in this book. Recipes for three cakes – vanilla sponge, chocolate sponge and carrot – are on pages 12–13. Buttercream icing is ideal for cake decorating and delicious to eat and royal icing is used for attaching decorations to cakes. Recipes are on pages 14–15.

Sugarpaste

Sugarpaste comes ready to use and is sold in blocks. Details on working with sugarpaste are on page 18. Working with sugarpaste requires cornflour for rolling it out or for dusting your cutting tools. Occasionally you'll find that sugarpaste has become too dry, so you can knead a little white fat into it to soften it.

Food Colourings & Decorations

For colouring sugarpaste, buttercream and royal icing, I like to use gel food colouring because the colours are more concentrated and I can create any shade I want.

Sometimes I use a thin coloured stain to obtain a more transparent colour. For example, a brown stain gives the look of real wood, so I mix a little

vodka with a food colouring to obtain the desired consistency. The alcohol evaporates quickly and will not dissolve the sugarpaste.

There are many wonderful edible decorations on the market. I often use dragées, small beads of sugar that come in silver, gold, copper or rainbow-coloured; alternatively, if these are not available, you can make the beads from sugarpaste, allow them to harden and cover with edible glitter, edible gold or silver leaf. Luster dust is an edible dust that can be brushed on dry to add sparkle or mixed with vodka to give a more intense sheen. If luster dust is not available you can substitute edible glitter to achieve the same effect. Petal dust is a matte edible dust that can be brushed on dry to enhance the colour of flowers or leaves or mixed with vodka to paint on details.

Other Supplies

You will occasionally need gum paste, for making flowers or any delicate decorations, such as feathers. When using gum paste, you'll need a bit of shortening because it can dry out quickly. Piping gel is used to adhere sugarpaste to cake drums and as a glaze to add sheen. 'Candy Melts' used for attaching decorations. All are available from cake decorating supply shops or online.

CAKE DECORATING TOOLS

Once you begin to decorate cakes, you'll find you need specific tools to make the process easier. The most important and common tools are described below, but you will also find others mentioned in the design projects in this book.

Cake Tins, Boards, Drums and Stands

Cake tins come in all shapes and sizes. I like to keep a wide range of metal tins on hand to have more to choose from. Cake boards are used under all cake layers. Cake drums are used to transport the cake. You will need them in several sizes and shapes. Finished cakes can be displayed on a decorated cake drum or a pretty cake stand.

Tools for Sugarpaste

Large rolling pins are used to roll out large pieces of sugarpaste to cover cakes. Small rolling pins are for smaller decoration pieces. Textured rolling pins have designs imprinted on them, which create fun designs. Sugarpaste smoothers will help to ease out wrinkles and any air pockets. Sugarcraft guns create shaped pieces of sugarpaste.

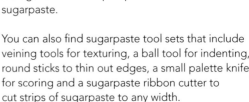
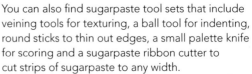

You can also find sugarpaste tool sets that include veining tools for texturing, a ball tool for indenting, round sticks to thin out edges, a small palette knife for scoring and a sugarpaste ribbon cutter to cut strips of sugarpaste to any width.

Knives

Knives are very useful in cake decorating. Large serrated knives are great for working on cakes – for levelling the tops, trimming the sides and for slicing a layer in half horizontally. Pizza cutters are handy for trimming excess sugarpaste from a cake. For more precise detailing, small, sharp knives and utility knives are essential.

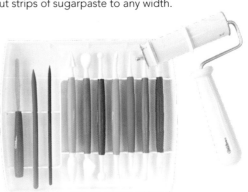

Design Tools and Cutters

Paintbrushes in several sizes are key tools for a variety of tasks; they'll help with the smallest details. A painter's palette is used for mixing colours. You can create amazing effects with an airbrush. It produces a very even coverage of colour. You can add all sorts of textures with different tools, such as a quilting tool. Flower formers help you dry sugar flowers in a more natural shape.

Cutters, mostly used for cutting sugarpaste shapes for decorations, can be found in all shapes and sizes in cake decorating supply shops. Circles, squares, diamonds, stars, hearts, letters, leaves, flowers and ovals abound. Having a large selection is useful as well as fun.

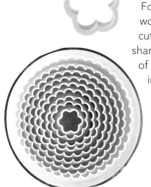

For stacking tiers, you'll need wooden dowels, which you'll cut with shears and a pencil sharpener to sharpen one end of the dowel. Dowels are sold in 6-mm (¼-inch) diameter at cake decorating supply shops. The ones sold at hardware shops are not

food-safe. Piping bags and assorted piping tips are used to add piped buttercream designs to your cake.

Other Useful Tools & Supplies

A turntable is helpful for holding the cake while you apply buttercream. Offset spatulas are wonderful for spreading buttercream icing over a cake. Use dough scrapers to smooth the buttercream before laying on the sugarpaste. Pastry brushes are used to apply piping gel to adhere sugarpaste to a cake drum. Baking trays, covered with parchment paper, are useful to hold pieces of sugarpaste as they dry. Cocktail sticks can help hold decorating pieces on the cake. Cling film is essential for wrapping sugarpaste when you're not using it. A thin piece of foam helps when you're working with some types of decorations.

BASIC RECIPES

Nothing is more disappointing than to cut into a beautiful cake and take your first bite only to find it dry and tasteless. I believe that a cake must taste as good as it looks. The following recipes have been perfected over the years and their moistness and flavour are guaranteed to please.

BATTER AMOUNT TO FILL CAKE TIN

15-cm (6-inch) tin – 510 g (1 lb 2 oz)   *25-cm (10-inch) tin – 1.4 kg (3 lbs)*

20-cm (8-inch) tin – 850 g (1 lb 14 oz)   *30-cm (12-inch) tin – 2 kg (4 lb 6 oz)*

VANILLA SPONGE
MAKES 6 CUPS 1KG (2LB 3OZ)

This classic recipe yields a versatile cake that can be paired with any type of filling. The addition of beaten egg whites gives the cake a light, airy texture, hence the name 'sponge' cake. To obtain this soft texture, avoid overmixing. Lightly folding in the egg whites will help to aerate the batter.

320 g (11 oz) fine plain flour
1½ tbsp. baking powder
1½ tsp. salt
240 ml (8 fl oz) whole milk
1 tsp. vanilla essence
250 g (8 oz) unsalted butter
300 g (10 oz) caster
  sugar
5 large egg whites

STEP 1
Preheat oven to 175°C (350°F). Generously grease two 20-cm (8-inch) cake tins. Set aside.

STEP 2
Sieve together the flour, baking powder and salt in a mixing bowl. In a separate bowl, stir together the milk and vanilla.

STEP 3
In the large mixing bowl, cream the butter and sugar together with a handheld mixer until pale in colour. Add the dry ingredients in three batches, alternating with the liquid ingredients. Begin and end with the dry ingredients. Mix until well combined.

STEP 4
Beat the egg whites to obtain stiff peaks. Gently fold into the batter. Do not overmix. Divide the batter between the prepared tins.

STEP 5
Bake for 45 minutes or until a wooden skewer inserted into the centre comes out clean. Remove from the oven and allow to cool in the tins on a rack.

CHOCOLATE SPONGE
MAKES 1 KG (2 LB 3 OZ)

The dark cocoa powder lends a good, rich flavour to this cake.

225 g (8 oz) fine plain flour
55 g p (2 oz) cocoa powder
1½ tbsp. baking powder
1½ tsp. salt
240 ml (8 fl oz) whole milk
1 tsp. vanilla essence
225 g (8 oz) unsalted butter
300 g (10 oz) caster sugar
5 large egg whites

STEP 1
Preheat oven to 175°C (350°F). Generously grease two 20-cm (8-inch) cake tins. Set aside.

STEP 2
Sieve together the flour, cocoa, baking powder and salt in a mixing bowl. In a separate bowl, stir together the milk and vanilla.

STEP 3
In a large mixing bowl, cream the butter and sugar together until pale in colour. Add the dry ingredients in three batches, alternating with the liquid ingredients. Begin and end with the dry ingredients. Mix until combined.

STEP 4
Beat the egg whites until stiff peaks form. Gently fold into the batter. Do not overmix. Divide the batter between the prepared tins.

STEP 5
Bake for 45 minutes or until a wooden skewer inserted into the centre comes out clean. Remove from the oven and allow to cool in the tins on a rack.

CARROT CAKE
MAKES 1 KG (2 LB 3 OZ)

The tangy buttermilk in this recipe makes this the most moist carrot cake you have ever tasted. When I pair it with our creamy buttercream, our customers cannot get enough of this classic cake.

270 g (9 ½ oz) fine plain flour
2 tbsp. baking powder
½ tsp. salt
1 tsp. ground cinnamon
450 g (1 lb) carrots, peeled and grated
3 large eggs
120 ml (4 fl oz) buttermilk
300 g (10 oz) caster sugar
240 ml (8 fl oz) vegetable oil
1 tsp. vanilla essence

STEP 1
Preheat oven to 175°C (350°F). Generously grease two 20-cm (8-inch) tins. Set aside.

STEP 2
Sieve the flour, baking powder, salt and cinnamon together into a mixing bowl.

STEP 3
In a separate bowl, mix together the grated carrots, eggs, buttermilk, sugar, oil and vanilla.

STEP 4
Gently fold the dry ingredients into the carrot mixture. Mix until combined. Divide the batter between the prepared tins.

STEP 5
Bake for 45 minutes or until a wooden skewer inserted into the centre comes out clean. Remove from the oven and allow to cool in the tins on a rack.

BUTTERCREAM ICING
MAKES 2 KG (4 LB 6 OZ)

Buttercream is a type of icing that is used inside cakes as a filling, outside as a coating and also for decorating. This recipe calls for butter to be added to whipped meringue, making an icing that is as light as whipped cream. Buttercream can be tinted with gel food colouring; mix in a very little at a time until the desired shade is obtained.

450 g (1 lb) caster sugar
12 large egg whites
1 kg (2lb 4 oz) unsalted butter,
cut into cubes
1 tsp. clear vanilla essence (available in cake decorating supply shops)

STEP 1
Mix together the sugar and egg whites in a heatproof bowl. Set over a pan of simmering water.

STEP 2
Beat with a hand-held mixer until the mixture reaches 60°C (140°F) and then immediately remove the bowl from the heat.

STEP 3
Continue beating with the mixer on high speed until the mixture forms stiff peaks.

STEP 4
Begin adding the butter, cube by cube. Beat until well combined and then add the vanilla and mix well again.

STEP 5
If not using immediately, keep it well covered in the refrigerator. It can be stored for up to a week, but keep it away from strong odours as it may absorb the odour.

ROYAL ICING
MAKES 450 G (1 LB)

Royal icing is a white icing that dries hard and is perfect for gluing decorations onto a cake. It crusts over quickly when left, so it needs to be wrapped tightly with cling film until ready to use. If you want to colour royal icing, use gel food colouring.

400 g (14 oz) icing sugar
2 large egg whites
1 tsp. freshly squeezed lemon juice

STEP 1
Sift the icing sugar into a bowl.

STEP 2
Using a hand-held or stationary mixer, beat in the egg whites and lemon juice. Continue beating until the icing holds its shape when you run a knife through it.

STEP 3
Cover the bowl with cling film to prevent the icing from drying out. Set aside until ready to use.

Royal icing can be used to embellish the cake as well as to attach sugarpaste decorations.

ESSENTIAL DECORATING TECHNIQUES

LEVELLING, SPLITTING AND FILLING CAKE LAYERS

STEP 1

After you have made your cakes, allow them to cool completely overnight in their tins to firm up the crumb, which will make the cakes easier to decorate.

STEP 2

Place a cake board of the same size and shape as the cake on top of a bigger cake drum. The drum should be at least 5 cm (2 inches) bigger than the cake for easy handling.

STEP 3

Place a dab of buttercream on the board to keep the cake from moving around. Remove one cake layer from its tin. Place it on the cake board, bottom-side down. Using a large serrated knife, level off the cake's rounded top. This will give the next tier a flat surface to sit on.

STEP 4

Now split the cake in half horizontally. Hold a large serrated knife against the side of the cake and applying gentle pressure, work the knife through the cake. Hold the knife steady so that the two halves are even. Lift off the top half and set it aside.

STEP 5

With an offset spatula, spread some buttercream over the bottom half. You want the buttercream filling to be about 8 mm (1/3 inch) thick and evenly spread right to the edge. Replace the top half. Place the cake on a turntable.

STEP 6

Apply a thin coat of buttercream to the top and the sides of the cake. Refrigerate until firm. This will seal in the crumbs and may take around 20 minutes.

STEP 7

Apply a second coat of buttercream to the top and sides of the cake. Holding a dough scraper flat against the side of the cake, turn the cake to remove the excess buttercream and smooth out the remaining buttercream. Refrigerate for 1 hour before decorating to allow the buttercream to firm up.

STEP 8

Repeat the process with each of the cake layers.

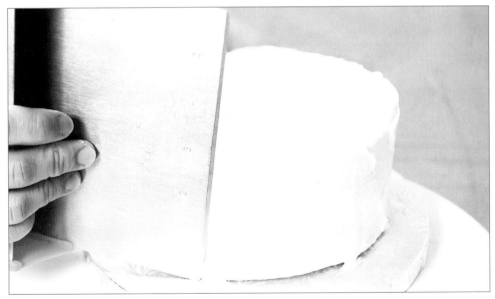

USING SUGARPASTE

STEP 1

Sugarpaste is applied after the buttercream is firm and acts as a great canvas for decorating a cake. It does not melt like buttercream and it provides many more decorating possibilities. Sugarpaste is also good for sealing in moisture, so it keeps the cake from drying out. The layer of buttercream underneath helps the sugarpaste adhere to the cake.

STEP 2

Sugarpaste must be soft and pliable and at room temperature so you can roll it out or colour it. Knead it with your hands, to warm it up, until it is fully pliable.

STEP 3

If you're using the sugarpaste in its basic colour – white – you're now ready to roll it out. Skip to step 5.

STEP 4

If you're colouring the sugarpaste, apply a little gel food colouring with a cocktail stick to the sugarpaste right after you knead it. It is better to add a little colouring at a time so that you can control the shade of the colour. Gel food colours are more concentrated and will not soften the sugarpaste too much, as liquid colours do. If the sugarpaste becomes sticky from the gel food colouring as you're kneading it in, dust your hands with cornflour.

When the desired colour is achieved, wrap the sugarpaste tightly with cling film and set aside until you are ready to use it. It is important to keep sugarpaste tightly wrapped and at room temperature to keep it from drying and cracking. Repeat until you've coloured all the sugarpaste you'll be using.

STEP 5

To roll out sugarpaste, take the amount of sugarpaste you will need to cover the sides and top of a cake. Dust your work surface with cornflour to keep the sugarpaste from sticking. Using a large rolling pin, roll out the sugarpaste to a 6 mm (¼ inch) thickness in the size you need. Remove air bubbles by pricking them with a straight pin to release the air. Make sure to continue dusting the work surface with cornflour as you roll.

STEP 6

Gently lift the sugarpaste by placing both hands underneath it and place it over the prepared cake tier.

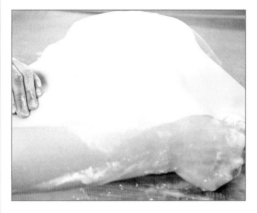

STEP 7

Ease out all wrinkles and air bubbles with your hands. Then use a sugarpaste smoother to smooth the top and sides.

STEP 8

Cut off the excess with a pizza cutter. Save any excess sugarpaste that has not touched the buttercream, wrap it tightly with cling film and set it aside for later use.

STEP 9

If you're using sugarpaste for individual decorations, roll it to a 3 mm (⅛ inch) thickness. You can now cut it with shaped cutters or a sugarpaste ribbon cutter, dusting the tools with cornflour as necessary. Sugarpaste decorations can be attached to a cake with a little water.

STEP 10

Sometimes sugarpaste is used to decorate a cake drum, to match the cake. The process is essentially the same – you're using 6 mm (¼ inch) thick sugarpaste. To trim off the excess, use a sharp knife.

STACKING CAKE TIERS

To make a tiered cake, you need to know how to stack and stabilise the tiers so they do not collapse under the weight of the tiers on top. You do this by inserting dowels into the lower tiers of a cake to bear the weight of the upper tiers. I like to use 6 mm (¼ inch) wide wooden dowels, which are sold in cake decorating supply shops (they're food-safe). You'll first need to cut them with shears or very strong scissors to the correct length.

The dowels need to be the exact same height as the cake tier they're going into and you'll need enough of them to support the weight of the next tier. (Each project in this book specifies how many dowels and what length you'll need.)

STEP 1

Start with the bottom tier, which you've set on a cake drum. Cut the rods needed for that tier according to the instructions given in the project.

STEP 2

Centre a cake board the same size as the tier above on the tier you wish to dowel. With a knife, lightly score the outline of the cake board. Remove the board. Working inside that outline, start inserting the dowels vertically into the cake, pushing them all the way down to the cake drum and spacing them evenly within the imprinted outline.

STEP 3

Place the cake board back on the cake; line it up with the outline. Centre the next tier, on its cake board, on the cake.

STEP 4

Repeat this process with every tier, except for the top tier.

STEP 5

The last step is to stabilise the tiers with an additional centre dowel to keep them from shifting. Cut one long dowel to the length indicated in the project. With a pencil sharpener (that you have never used to sharpen a pencil), sharpen one end of the rod. Drive the rod, sharp end down, through the centre of the cake all the way to the cake drum. To do this, you may need to hit it with a small hammer. Dab on some royal icing to hide the hole in the top of the cake.

VIOLET SCROLLS

The simple, timeless scrollwork in this design makes it a classic. Keep it to one
tier for a small gathering or repeat the steps on several tiers for a large affair.

TOOLS

- serrated knife
- offset spatula
- 20-cm (8-inch) round
  cake board
- dough scraper
- rolling pin
- sugarpaste smoother
- pizza cutter
- 25-cm (10-inch) round
  cake drum
- textured rolling pin
- sugarpaste ribbon cutter
- piping bag and coupler
- #3 piping tip
- stencil with scroll design

MATERIALS

- two (20-cm/8-inch) round
  carrot cakes (5 cm/
  2 inches high)
- 560 g (1 lb 3 oz) buttercream
- 700 g (1 lb 9 oz) white
  sugarpaste
- gel food colouring – violet
- cornflour
- royal icing

OVERVIEW

All steps can be completed in one day.

- Make the two cakes and
  set aside to cool (approx.
  1 hr)
- Level, split, fill and
  assemble the two cakes
  (½ hr)
- Cover with buttercream
  (1½ hrs including
  refrigeration)
- Cover cake with
  sugarpaste (½ hr)
- Attach the imprinted
  sugarpaste (10 mins)
- Pipe the deep violet royal
  icing along the imprinted
  lines (½ hr)
- Stencil the top of the
  cake (½ hr)

two (20-cm/8-inch)
round carrot cakes
(5 cm/2 inches high)

STEP 1

Level the tops of the 20-cm (8-inch) cakes, split in half horizontally, and fill between the layers with buttercream. Place the 20-cm (8-inch) tier on the 20-cm (8-inch) cake board. Cover with a thin layer of buttercream. Refrigerate for 20 minutes. Cover the top and sides with a second, thicker coat of buttercream. Smooth with the dough scraper and refrigerate for 1 hour.

STEP 2

Reserve 30 grams (1 ounce) white sugarpaste. Dye the rest light violet. Roll out to 6 mm (¼ inch) thick on a cornflour-covered surface and cover the cake. Smooth with the sugarpaste smoother and trim the excess with the pizza cutter. Transfer the cake to the cake drum, adding a dab of royal icing to hold the cake in place.

STEP 3

Roll out the reserved sugarpaste to 3 mm (⅛ inch) thick. Gently roll over the sugarpaste with the textured rolling pin to give it a scroll design.

STEP 4

Using the sugarpaste ribbon cutter, cut out a strip of sugarpaste 1 cm (½ inch) wide and long enough to wrap around the sides of the cake.

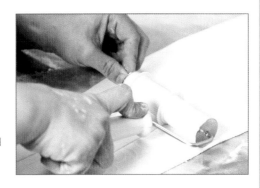

STEP 5

Attach the strip to the base of the cake with a little water.

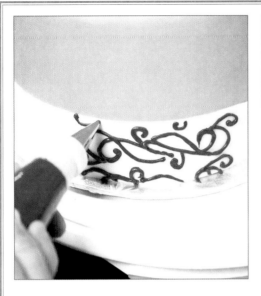

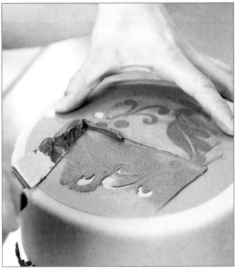

STEP 6

Dye 110 grams (4 ounces) of royal icing deep violet. Fill the piping bag and attach the #3 piping tip. Pipe along the imprinted lines of the white sugarpaste strip by holding the tip at a 45-degree angle to the cake and moving the tip downward as you apply pressure.

STEP 7

Place the stencil on top of the cake. Hold it still, and with a small offset spatula, spread a thin layer of deep violet royal icing over the stencil. Scrape off the excess. Gently lift off the stencil, without smudging the design.

CUBE

The versatility of this cake design makes it appropriate for people of all ages.
Enjoy playing around with the colours and sizes of the dots.

TOOLS

- pastry brush
- rolling pin
- 25-cm (10-inch) square cake drum
- sharp knife
- clingfilm
- serrated knife
- offset spatula
- 15-cm (6-inch) square cake board
- dough scraper
- sugarpaste smoother
- pizza cutter
- 3 small round cutters in varying sizes
- ruler
- #12 piping tip
- black-and-grey striped ribbon
- glue stick

MATERIALS

- piping gel
- 850 g (30 oz) white sugarpaste
- gel food colouring – black
- two (15-cm/6-inch) square vanilla cakes (5 cm/ 2 inches high)
- 350 g (12 oz) buttercream
- cornflour
- royal icing

OVERVIEW

All steps can be completed in one day.

- Cover the cake drum with black sugarpaste

- Make the two cakes and set aside to cool (approx. 1 hr)

- Level, split, fill and assemble the two cakes (½ hr)

- Cover with buttercream (1½ hrs including refrigeration)

- Cover cake with sugarpaste (½ hr)

- Cut out the dots and attach them to the cake (1 hr)

two (15-cm/6-inch) square vanilla cakes (5 cm/2 inches high)

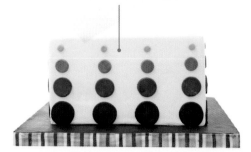

STEP 1

Spread piping gel evenly over the cake drum with the pastry brush. Dye 280 grams (10 ounces) of the sugarpaste black, roll it out to 6 mm (¼ inch) thick and cover the cake drum. Trim the excess with the sharp knife. Set the trimmings aside and cover with clingfilm.

STEP 2

Level the tops of each cake layer with the serrated knife, split them in half horizontally and fill between each layer with buttercream. Stack the cakes on the 15-cm (6-inch) cake board. Spread with a thin coat of buttercream and refrigerate for 20 minutes. Cover with a second, thicker coat of buttercream and smooth it with the dough scraper. Refrigerate for 1 hour.

STEP 3

Roll out the rest of the white sugarpaste to 6 mm (¼ inch) thick and cover the cake. Smooth with the sugarpaste smoother and trim off the excess with the pizza cutter. Transfer the covered cake to the prepared cake drum. Secure with a dab of royal icing.

STEP 4

Roll out the leftover black sugarpaste you set aside to 3 mm (⅛ inch) thick and cut out 16 dots with the biggest cutter.

STEP 5

Place the ruler against the base of the cake and mark at 2.5-cm (1-inch) intervals. Repeat on all sides. Attach the black dots with a little water within these 2.5-cm (1-inch) intervals.

STEP 6

Mix the scraps of black sugarpaste with an equal part of white sugarpaste to make a dark grey.

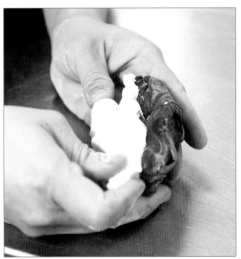

STEP 7

Roll out to 3 mm (⅛ inch) thick and cut 16 dots with the second-largest cutter.

STEP 8

Attach each dot directly above the black dot along the sides of the cake with a little water. You will now have two horizontal rows of dots.

STEP 9

Mix the remaining dark grey sugarpaste with an equal part of white sugarpaste to make a light grey colour. Roll out to 3 mm (⅛ inch) thick and cut 16 dots with the smallest cutter. Attach these dots directly above the last row of dark grey dots.

STEP 10

Finally, mix the remaining light grey sugarpaste with an equal part of white sugarpaste to make a lighter grey colour. Roll out to 3 mm (⅛ inch) thickness and cut 16 dots with the #12 piping tip. Attach these dots directly above the last row of light grey dots.

STEP 11

Attach the ribbon to the cake drum with the glue stick.

JAPANESE-INSPIRED TEA CAKE

Inspiration for cake designs can come from all places. In this case, it comes in the form of a teapot. The delicate painted leaves and sugar bamboo against the fresh green makes this cake perfect for a spring celebration.

TOOLS

- 23-cm (9-inch) hexagon cake tin
- 25-cm (10-inch) round cake board
- scissors
- serrated knife
- offset spatula
- dough scraper
- rolling pin
- sugarpaste smoother
- pizza cutter
- small palette knife
- painter's palette
- small paintbrushes and a big paintbrush
- small knife

MATERIALS

- two (23-cm/9-inch) hexagon carrot cakes (2 inches/ 5 cm high)
- 1 kg (2¼ lb) buttercream
- 2.5 kg (5½ lb) white sugarpaste
- food colouring – leaf green, chocolate brown, lemon yellow and ivory
- royal icing
- brown petal dust
- vodka
- cornflour
- small teapot to decorate top of cake

OVERVIEW

All steps can be completed in one day.

- Make the two cakes and set aside to cool (approx. 1 hr)

- Level, split, fill and assemble the two cakes (½ hr)

- Cover with buttercream (1½ hrs, including refrigeration)

- Cover cake with sugarpaste (½ hr)

- Prepare, make and attach the sugarpaste 'bamboo' pieces to the cake (1½ hrs)

- Paint the sides of the cake (1 hr)

- Final touches and additional decorations (1 hr)

two (9-inch/ 23-cm) hexagon carrot cakes (2 inches/ 5 cm high)

STEP 1

Place the hexagon tin on top of the cake board and trace. Cut out the hexagon.

STEP 2

Level and split both hexagon cake layers and place on the hexagon cake board. Fill the layers with buttercream to get a 10-cm (4-inch) tall cake tower. Cover the top and sides with a thin layer of buttercream and refrigerate for 20 minutes. Spread a thicker layer of buttercream over the entire cake and smooth with the dough scraper. Chill for 1 hour.

STEP 3

Mix a small amount of the green, brown and yellow food colourings into 1 kg (35 oz) of the white sugarpaste. Knead the sugarpaste until you have a light pastel green colour.

STEP 4

Roll out the light green sugarpaste to 6 mm (¼ inch) thick and cover the hexagon-shaped cake. Smooth with the sugarpaste smoother and trim the excess with the pizza cutter.

STEP 5

Using the small palette knife, gently score horizontal lines across the sides and top of the cake to give it a textured look.

STEP 6

Dye the remaining white sugarpaste light brown. Measure out ½-teaspoon pieces of sugarpaste. Using your fingers, roll each piece into 4 cm (1½ inch) long logs. Make sure you roll the centre thinner than the ends. Holding each log on the vertical, lightly tap one end then the other against your work surface to flatten both ends.

STEP 7

Use a small paintbrush to dust brown petal dust over each end of the 'bamboo' pieces. Attach the bamboo pieces to the edges of the cake with royal icing. Trim them if they are too long.

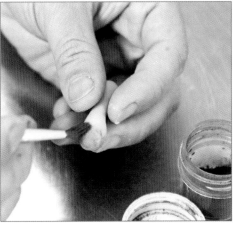

STEP 8

Mix the brown and green food colourings on the painter's palette and dilute with the vodka. With a fine-tipped brush, paint branches and leaves on the sides of the cake.

STEP 9

Dilute the colour with some more vodka and lightly paint the edges of each side.

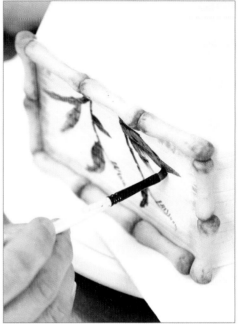

STEP 10

Make a diluted wash with the ivory food colouring and the vodka. Paint the top of the cake with a large brush. Decorate the teapot as desired and place it on the top of the cake when all the elements are dry.

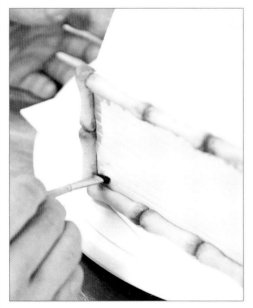

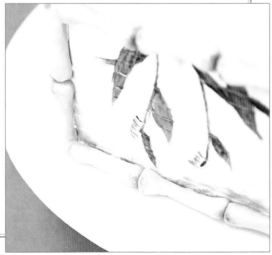

BLACK & WHITE RIBBONS

Contemporary designs call for sharp contrast and clean lines.
The unique feature of this cake is the unusual heights of its tiers.

TOOLS

- 15-cm (6-inch) round cake board
- two (20-cm/8-inch) round cake boards
- serrated knife
- offset spatula
- clingfilm
- dowels and shears
- 25-cm (10-inch) round cake board
- dough scraper
- rolling pin
- sugarpaste smoother
- pizza cutter
- pencil sharpener
- 30-cm (12-inch) round cake drum
- clothing steamer
- big paintbrush

MATERIALS

- two (15-cm/6-inch) round vanilla cakes (5 cm/2 inches high)
- one (20-cm/8-inch) round vanilla cake (5 cm/2 inches high)
- three (25-cm/10-inch) round vanilla cakes (5 cm/2 inches high)
- 1.9 kg (4¼ lb) buttercream
- 2.5 kg (5¾ lb) white sugarpaste
- gel food colouring – black
- cornflour
- royal icing
- 8-cm (3-inch) wide black plastic ribbon

OVERVIEW

All steps can be completed in one day.

- Make the six cakes and set aside to cool (approx. 3 hrs)
- Level, split, fill and assemble each tier (1½ hrs)
- Cover all tiers with buttercream (2 hrs including refrigeration)
- Cover all tiers with sugarpaste (1½ hrs)
- Insert dowels and assemble the tiers (½ hr)
- Attach ribbon to the bottom and top tiers (45 mins)

two 15-cm/ (6-inch) round vanilla cakes (5 cm/2 inches high)

one 20-cm/ (8-inch) round vanilla cake (5 cm/2 inches high)

three (25-cm/ 10-inch) round vanilla cakes (5 cm/2 inches high)

STEP 1

Prepare each of the two top tiers (the 15-cm/6-inch and the 20-cm/8-inch), on its corresponding cake board by levelling the tops, splitting the layers in half horizontally and filling between the layers with buttercream. Cover the bottom tier with a thin layer of buttercream. You will have one 10-cm (4-inch) high, 15-cm (6-inch) round tier and one 5-cm (2-inch) high 20-cm (8-inch) round tier.

STEP 2

For the 25-cm (10-inch) tier, level the tops and split all three cake rounds in half horizontally. Fill between the layers with buttercream. Stack just two of the cake rounds on the 25-cm (10-inch) cake board (it's now four layers of cake).

STEP 3

Cut six 10-cm (4-inch) long dowels.

STEP 4

Insert the dowels vertically into the filled 25-cm (10-inch) cake. Spread a layer of buttercream over the top of the cake.

STEP 5

Place the remaining 20-cm (8-inch) round board in the centre of the 25-cm (10-inch) tier. This will add support to the cake. Continue filling with buttercream and stacking the remaining 25-cm (10-inch) cake rounds. The result is a 25-cm (10-inch) tier measuring 6 inches (15 cm) in height. Spread a thin layer of buttercream over all three tiers. Refrigerate for 20 minutes. Cover the top and sides with a second, thicker coat of buttercream. Smooth with the dough scraper and refrigerate for 1 hour.

STEP 6

Dye 575 grams (20 ounces) of the white sugarpaste black. On a cornflour-covered surface, roll the black sugarpaste out to 6 mm (¼ inch) thick and cover the 20-cm (8-inch) round tier. Smooth with the sugarpaste smoother and trim the excess with the pizza cutter. Cover the trimmings with clingfilm and set aside.

STEP 7

Cut six 5-cm (2-inch) long dowels and eight 15-cm (6-inch) long dowels. Roll out the rest of the white sugarpaste to ¼ inch (6 mm) thick and cover the 15-cm (6-inch) and 25-cm (10-inch) round tiers. Smooth with the sugarpaste smoother and trim the excess with the pizza cutter. Insert the 5-cm (2-inch) long dowels vertically into the 20-cm (8-inch) tier. Leave a small space of 5 cm (2 inches) from the edge.

STEP 8

Insert the eight 15-cm (6-inch) long dowels vertically into the 25-cm (10-inch) tier. Place the 25-cm (10-inch) tier on the cake drum, securing it with a dab of royal icing. Place a dab of royal icing on top of the dowels. Place the 20-cm (8-inch) tier on top of the 25-cm (10-inch) tier. Then place the 15-cm (6-inch) tier on top of the 20-cm (8-inch) tier. Sharpen one end of a 30-cm (12-inch) long dowel. Drive it vertically through the centre of all three tiers. Cover the hole on top with royal icing.

STEP 9

With your fingers, shred the plastic ribbon. It will not shred evenly – there will be longer and shorter pieces, some thick and some thin. This will create a stunning effect.

STEP 10

Using a clothing steamer, steam all the tiers to produce a shiny finish.

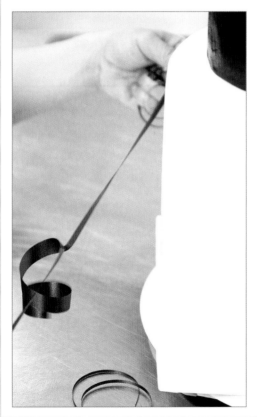

STEP 11

With a large paintbrush, wet the bottom half of the 15-cm (6-inch) tier and the bottom third of the 25-cm (10-inch) tier.

STEP 12

Encircle the wet sides of both tiers with the shredded ribbon, crisscrossing the ribbon. Steam again if desired.

RIBBON ROSES

This fresh and pretty three-tiered cake evokes the feeling of spring. You'll need to begin preparing the roses one day in advance to give them adequate drying time.

TOOLS

- parchment paper
- pencil and ruler
- scissors
- three piping bags and couplers
- 3 #102 piping tips
- #7 flower nail
- baking trays
- serrated knife
- 15-cm (6-inch) round cake board
- 20-cm (8-inch) round cake board
- 25-cm (10-inch) round cake board
- offset spatula
- dough scraper
- rolling pin
- sugarpaste smoother
- pizza cutter
- dowels and shears
- cake plate
- pencil sharpener

MATERIALS

- 1.3 kg (2 lb 14 oz) royal icing
- gel food colouring – golden yellow, brown, ivory
- two (15-cm/6-inch) round vanilla cakes (5 cm/ 2 inches high)
- two (20-cm/8-inch) round vanilla cakes (5 cm/ 2 inches high)
- two (25-cm/10-inch) round vanilla cakes (5 cm/ 2 inches high)
- 1.8 kg (4 lb) buttercream
- 2.2 kg (4 lb 14 oz) white sugarpaste
- cornflour, for dusting

OVERVIEW

This cake will require two days to complete.

DAY ONE
- Prepare the royal icing roses in order to allow adequate drying time.

DAY TWO
- Make the six cakes and set aside to cool (approx. 3 hrs)

- Level, split, fill and assemble each tier (1½ hrs)

- Cover all tiers with buttercream (2 hrs, including refrigeration)

- Cover all tiers with sugarpaste (1½ hrs)

- Insert dowels and assemble the tiers (½ hr)

- Attach the dried roses to the bottom and top tiers (45 mins)

two (15-cm/ 6-inch) round vanilla cakes (5 cm/2 inches high)

two 20-cm/ (8-inch) round vanilla cakes (5 cm/2 inches high)

two 25-cm/ (10-inch) round vanilla cakes (5 cm/2 inches high)

STEP 1

Cut parchment paper into 5-cm (2-inch) squares. You'll be making several hundred roses, enough to cover the cake tiers and each parchment square will hold a rose while it dries, so cut several hundred squares of parchment.

STEP 2

Fill one piping bag fitted with a #102 tip with 450 grams (1 lb) of white royal icing.

STEP 3

Dye 550 grams (20 oz) of royal icing with yellow, brown and ivory food colourings to create a muted golden-yellow colour. Fill a second piping bag fitted with a #102 tip with 450 grams (16 oz) of that yellow icing.

STEP 4

Add the remaining white royal icing to the remaining 110 grams (4 oz) of the yellow icing to make a lighter shade of yellow. Fill the last piping bag.

STEP 5

Starting with the muted golden-yellow icing, glue a square of parchment to the flower nail with a dab of icing. Hold the bag at a 45-degree angle to the flower nail. As you squeeze out the icing, twirl the nail clockwise with your thumb and forefinger to form a rose. Stop twirling when the rose is the size you want.

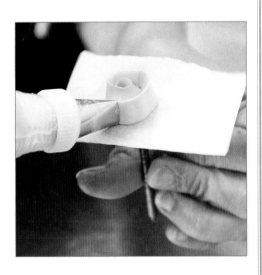

STEP 9

Dye the rest of the white sugarpaste with the yellow, brown and ivory food colourings to get a muted golden-yellow that matches the darker roses. Roll out to 6 mm (¼ inch) thick and cover the 15-cm (6-inch) tier. Smooth with the sugarpaste smoother and trim off the excess. Repeat with the 25-cm (10-inch) tier.

STEP 6

Gently lift off the parchment square and place it on the baking tray. Make roses of varying sizes until all the yellow icing is gone. Repeat with the lighter shade of yellow icing and the white icing. Let the roses dry overnight on the baking trays.

ASSEMBLING CAKE

STEP 7

Level the top of each 15-cm (6-inch) round and then split them in half horizontally, creating a total of four layers. Fill between each layer with buttercream and stack the four layers on the 15-cm (6-inch) cake board to create a 10-cm (4-inch) tall tower. Spread a thin coat of buttercream on the top and the sides. Refrigerate for 20 minutes, until it is firm. Spread a thicker coat of buttercream on the top and the sides. Smooth with the dough scraper. Refrigerate for 1 hour, until firm. Repeat these steps for the 20-cm (8-inch) and 25-cm (10-inch) rounds. Place each tier on its corresponding cake board.

STEP 8

Roll out 675 grams (24 ounces) of white sugarpaste to 6 mm (¼ inch) thick. Cover the 20-cm (8-inch) tier. Smooth with the sugarpaste smoother and trim excess with the pizza cutter.

STEP 10

Cut the dowels into fourteen 10-cm (4-inch) long pieces. Insert eight dowels vertically into the 25-cm (10-inch) tier and six dowels into the 20-cm (8-inch) tier. Space the dowels evenly. Place the 25-cm (10-inch) tier on the cake plate and stack the 20-cm (8-inch) tier on top. Stack the 6-inch (15-cm) tier on top of the 20-cm (8-inch) tier. Sharpen one end of a 30-cm (12-inch) long dowel and drive it vertically through the centre of all three tiers. Cover the hole on top with a dab of dark yellow royal icing.

STEP 11

Using small dabs of royal icing, attach the dried ribbon roses to the side of the 15-cm (6-inch) and 25-cm (10-inch) tiers. Alternate colours and sizes of roses.

COSMOPOLITAN

There is always an allure of excitement about New York City. This modern three-tiered cake pays tribute to the Big Apple and is perfect for a bridal shower.

TOOLS

- serrated knife
- 15-cm (6-inch) round cake board
- 18-cm (7-inch) round cake board
- 20-cm (8-inch) round cake board
- offset spatula
- dough scraper
- rolling pin
- sugarpaste smoother
- pizza cutter
- cling film
- dowels and shears
- pencil sharpener
- airbrush and compressor
- utility knife
- baking tray
- parchment paper
- paintbrushes
- piping bag and coupler
- #2 piping tip
- letter cutters ('I', 'N', 'Y')
- heart-shaped cutter

MATERIALS

- two (15-cm/6-inch) round vanilla cakes (5 cm/2 inches high)
- two (18-cm/7-inch) round vanilla cakes (5 cm/2 inches high)
- two (20-cm/8-inch) round vanilla cakes (5 cm/2 inches high)
- 1.2 kg (2 lb 10 oz) buttercream
- 1.8 kg (4 lb) white sugarpaste
- cornflour
- airbrush colours – pink, Hawaiian blue, black
- royal icing
- gel food colouring – black, red

OVERVIEW

All steps can be completed in one day.

- Make the six cakes and set aside to cool (approx. 3 hrs)

- Level, split, fill and assemble tiers (1½ hrs)

- Cover all tiers with buttercream (1½ hrs, including refrigeration)

- Cover all tiers with sugarpaste (1½ hrs)

- Insert dowels and assemble tiers (½ hr)

- Spray the cake with pink, blue and black airbrush colours (½ hr)

- Prepare and make the sugarpaste buildings and letters (approx. 2 hrs, including drying time)

- Attach sugarpaste buildings and letters to the cake (½ hr)

two (15-cm/6-inch) round vanilla cakes (5 cm/2 inches high)

two (18-cm/7-inch) round vanilla cakes (5 cm/2 inches high)

two (20-cm/8-inch) round vanilla cakes (5 cm/2 inches high)

STEP 1

Level the top of each 15-cm (6-inch) round and then split them in half horizontally with the serrated knife, creating a total of four layers. Fill between each layer with buttercream and stack the four layers on the 15-cm (6-inch) cake board to make a 10-cm (4-inch) tall tower. Spread a thin coat of buttercream on the top and the sides. Refrigerate for 20 minutes, until it is firm. Spread a thicker coat of buttercream on the top and the sides. Smooth with the dough scraper and refrigerate for 1 hour, until firm. Repeat these steps for the 18-cm (7-inch) and 20-cm (8-inch) rounds. Place each tier on its corresponding cake board.

STEP 2

Roll out the white sugarpaste to 6 mm (¼ inch) thick. Cover the 15-cm (6-inch) tier. Smooth with the sugarpaste smoother and trim off the excess with the pizza cutter. Wrap the trimmings in clingfilm and set aside. Repeat with the 18-cm (7-inch) and 20-cm (8-inch) tiers.

STEP 3

Cut the dowels into twelve 10-cm (4-inch) long pieces. Leave one dowel 30 cm (12 inches) long and sharpen one end. Insert six dowels vertically into the 20-cm (8-inch) tier and six into the 18-cm (7-inch) tier. Space them evenly. Stack the 18-cm (7-inch) tier on top of the 20-cm (8-inch) tier and the 15-cm (6-inch) on top of the 18-cm (7-inch) tier. Drive the 30-cm (12-inch) dowel vertically through the centre of all the tiers. Cover the hole on top with a dab of royal icing.

STEP 4

Fill the airbrush with the pink airbrush colour. Spray pink onto the edges of the tiers, fading it out toward the middle of each tier. Lightly spray blue and black airbrush colours on top of the pink.

STEP 5

Roll out the remaining sugarpaste to 6 mm (¼ inch) thick. With the utility knife, cut out building shapes, varying the sizes and heights of the buildings.

STEP 6

Place the shapes on a baking tray lined with parchment paper. Lightly airbrush with pink and blue colours. It looks best when the colours overlap slightly. Airbrush the edges with black. Allow to dry for 1 hour.

STEP 7

With a paintbrush, wet each 'building' lightly with water on the unpainted side. Attach them to the top and bottom cake tiers. Overlap the buildings slightly and vary the heights of the buildings. With white royal icing in the piping bag and the #2 tip, pipe rows of dots to make windows.

STEP 8

Dye 30 grams (1 ounce) of sugarpaste black and 30 grams (1 ounce) of sugarpaste red. Roll the black out to 3 mm (⅛ inch) thick. Cut out the letters 'I' and 'N' and 'Y'. Roll out the red sugarpaste to 3 mm (⅛ inch) thick. Cut out a medium-sized heart. Attach the message 'I ♥ NY' to the side of the middle tier with a little water.

GIFT BOX

The gift box is one of the most popular designs that we have seen over the years. You can change the colours, the polka dots to stripes, or the loopy bow to a traditional tied-up bow. Now you can have your gift and eat it too.

TOOLS

- pastry brush
- 20-cm (8-inch) square cake drum
- rolling pin
- sharp kitchen knife
- serrated knife
- baking tray
- parchment paper
- sugarpaste ribbon cutter
- cocktail sticks
- small paintbrush
- 15-cm (6-inch) square cake board
- offset spatula
- dough scraper
- sugarpaste smoother
- pizza cutter
- scissors
- small and medium circle cutters
- piping bag and coupler
- #16 piping tip
- 2 cm (¾-inch) wide brown satin ribbon
- glue stick

MATERIALS

- piping gel
- 2 kg (4¼ lb) white sugarpaste
- gel food colouring – leaf green, chocolate brown, lemon yellow
- shortening
- cornflour
- two (15-cm/6-inch) square chocolate cakes (5 cm/ 2 inches high)
- 475 g (17 oz) buttercream
- royal icing

OVERVIEW

This cake will require two days to complete.

DAY ONE
- Prepare and cover the cake drum (½ hr)

- Prepare and make the sugarpaste loops (1 hr)

DAY TWO
- Make the two cakes and set aside to cool (approx. 1 hr)

- Level, split, fill and assemble the cake (1 hr)

- Cover the cake with buttercream (1½ hrs, including refrigeration)

- Cover with sugarpaste (1 hr)

- Prepare, make and attach the sugarpaste ribbons to the cake (½ hr)

- Cut out and attach the circles and dots (45 mins)

- Pipe royal icing along base of cake (10 mins)

- Assemble the bow with the sugarpaste loops and attach to the top of the cake (½ hr)

two (15-cm/ 6-inch) square chocolate cakes (5 cm/2 inches high)

STEP 1

With the pastry brush, brush the cake drum with piping gel. Make sure to cover the surface completely so the sugarpaste can adhere. With the rolling pin, roll out 510 grams (18 ounces) of the white sugarpaste to 6 mm (¼ inch) thick and cover the cake drum. Trim the sides with the kitchen knife and keep the trimmings with the rest of the white sugarpaste. Set the cake drum aside to dry.

STEP 2

Cover the baking tray with parchment paper.

STEP 3

Mix the leaf green, chocolate brown and lemon-yellow gel colours into 750 grams (26 ounces) of the white sugarpaste to achieve a sage-green colour. Colour 310 grams (11 ounces) of the white sugarpaste a deep chocolate brown. Leave the rest white. Set aside 675 grams (24 ounces) of the sage green to cover the cake.

STEP 4

Grease a working surface with a little shortening. With the rolling pin, roll each of the green, brown and white sugarpastes into a 3 mm(⅛ inch) thick sheet. Using the sugarpaste ribbon cutter, cut eight 2-cm (¾inch) strips measuring 20 cm (8 inches) long from each sheet. Cover remaining strips with clingfilm and reserve.

STEP 5

Fold the sugarpaste to form the loops. Break 12 cocktail sticks in half. With the paintbrush, wet the lower third of each sugarpaste strip with a little water.

STEP 6

Lightly press one of the halved cocktail sticks into the wet part of a sugarpaste strip, leaving half of the stick hanging off. Fold the strip over and pinch the two ends together so that the cocktail stick will not fall out. Set the loop on its side on the prepared baking tray. Use your fingers to shape it into a rounded loop.

STEP 7

Repeat with all the sugarpaste strips. There will be extra loops in case of breakage. Set aside to dry on the baking tray overnight.

DECORATING THE GIFT BOX
STEP 8

Trim the tops of both cake layers with the serrated knife to achieve a level surface. Split each layer in half horizontally. Place both halves of one of the split layers on the cake board. Remove its top half. Using the offset spatula, spread 40 grams (1½ oz) of buttercream on the layer. Replace the top half of this layer. Spread the top with 40 grams (1½ oz) of buttercream. Repeat with the remaining cake layer and stack it, bottom-side up, on top of the other cake layer. Cover the top and sides of the cake tower with a thin coating of buttercream. Refrigerate until firm and then apply a second coat of buttercream and smooth with a dough scraper. Refrigerate for 1 hour, until firm. Roll out the reserved 680-gram (24-ounce) piece of green sugarpaste to 6mm (¼ inch) thick.

STEP 9

Cover the prepared cake tower in the green sugarpaste. Smooth all sides with the sugarpaste smoother and pinch the edges with your fingers to get nice, sharp corners.

STEP 10

Trim the excess with scissors and use a pizza cutter to trim around the cake. Transfer the covered cake onto the prepared cake drum, securing it with a dab of royal icing.

STEP 11

Roll out the remaining white sugarpaste to 6mm (½ inch) thick. Cut out two strips, each 1½ inches (4 cm) wide and 16 inches (40 cm) long. Roll up each strip. This will make it easier to apply them to the cake.

STEP 12

Using the paintbrush, wet the strips with a little water. Beginning on one side of the cake, apply the sugarpaste strip to the centre, rolling your way up the side, across the top and down the opposite side. Trim off the excess with the pizza cutter.

STEP 14

Roll out thinly any remaining white sugarpaste and then cut out circles with the medium circle cutter. With the small circle cutter, cut out the centre of the medium circles.

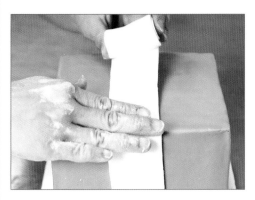

STEP 13

Repeat on the opposite side with the other strip. With your fingers, pinch the sugarpaste together at the point where the two strips cross to simulate a real ribbon.

STEP 15

Moisten with the wet paintbrush and apply the medium circles randomly to the gift box. Repeat with the small white circles.

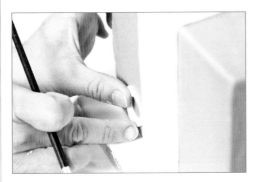

STEP 16

Thinly roll out the remaining brown sugarpaste and cut out small round dots. Moisten the brown dots and apply to all the medium circles with the cut-out centres. Using the pastry bag and #16 pastry tip, pipe white royal icing all along the base of the gift box.

STEP 17

Roll a ½-inch (1-cm) ball of leftover green sugarpaste. Insert the cocktail stick ends of a dried sugarpaste loop into the green ball of sugarpaste. Working with one loop at a time and alternating the colours, cover the entire ball. The result will be a bow with white, brown and green loops.

STEP 18

Gently lift the bow and secure it to the top of the gift box with some more royal icing.

RUFFLED BROOCH

This miniature cake proves that the old can be mixed with the new – with stunning results. Traditional ruffles and a cameo brooch are modernised by the graduated salmon tones.

TOOLS

- serrated knife
- offset spatula
- 13-cm (5-inch) round cake board
- 15-cm (6-inch) round cake board
- dough scraper
- small and large rolling pins
- sugarpaste smoother
- pizza cutter
- clingfilm
- medium oval cutter
- paintbrush
- 20-cm (8-inch) round cake drum
- dowels and shears
- cameo mould
- piece of thin foam
- rounded stick

MATERIALS

- two (13-cm/5-inch) round vanilla cakes (5 cm/ 2 inches high)
- two (15-cm/6-inch) round vanilla cakes (5 cm/ 2 inches high)
- 675 g (1¼ lb) buttercream
- 2 kg (4 lb 6 oz) ivory sugarpaste
- gel food colouring – red, orange, brown
- cornflour
- royal icing

OVERVIEW

This cake can be completed in one day due to its small size. For a larger version, allot yourself at least two days to cover completely with ruffles.

- Make the four cakes and set aside to cool (approx. 2 hrs)
- Level, split, fill and assemble the tiers (1 hr)
- Cover each tier with buttercream (1½ hrs, including refrigeration)
- Cover the tiers with sugarpaste and assemble (1 hr)
- Prepare, make and attach the sugarpaste ruffles to the bottom tier and to the top of the cake (approx. 2½ hrs)
- Make and attach the brooch (15 mins)

two 13-cm/(5-inch) round vanilla cakes (5 cm/2 inches high)

two (15-cm/6-inch) round vanilla cakes (5 cm/2 inches high)

56
RUFFLED BROOCH

STEP 1

Prepare the tiers – each on its corresponding cake board – by levelling the tops of each cake round, splitting them horizontally and filling between each layer with buttercream. Cover each tier with a thin layer of buttercream and refrigerate for 20 minutes. Cover with a second, thicker coat of buttercream and smooth with the dough scraper. Chill for 1 hour.

STEP 2

Roll out 1 kg (40 ounces) of the ivory sugarpaste to 6 mm (¼ inch) thick and cover the tiers. Smooth with the sugarpaste smoother and trim the excess with the pizza cutter.

STEP 3

Measure out 150 grams (5 ounces) of the ivory sugarpaste. Mix in red, orange and brown food colouring to dye it a dark salmon colour. Roll out to 3 mm (⅛ inch) thick. Using the medium oval cutter, cut out oval pieces.

STEP 4

Hold one oval piece in your hand and use your fingers to pinch the top half of the oval together to make a ruffled piece.

STEP 5

With a wet paintbrush, wet the ruffle piece and apply it to the base of the 15-cm (6-inch) tier. Repeat, attaching the ruffle pieces closely side by side, until the entire base is covered. Set the 15-cm (6-inch) tier aside and begin to cover the top edge of the 13-cm (5-inch) tier with more ruffles. The result will be a ring of dark salmon-coloured ruffles, with the ruffles all facing out.

STEP 6

Mix an equal amount of ivory sugarpaste with the remaining dark salmon sugarpaste to lighten the colour. Roll out to 6mm (⅛ inch) thick and cut out ovals. Pinch the top half of the oval to make a ruffle. Continue mixing the sugarpaste, creating lighter coloured sugarpastes each time by mixing equal parts ivory sugarpaste with the coloured sugarpastes, cutting out ovals and creating ruffles.

STEP 7

Attach each new colour of ruffles to the tiers, working from bottom to top on the 15-cm (6-inch) tier and outside to inside on the top of the 13-cm (5-inch) tier. Leave a 13-cm (5-inch) diameter space on the top of the 15-cm (6-inch) tier. This is where the 13-cm (5-inch) tier will sit.

STEP 8

Place the 15-cm (6-inch) tier on top of the 20-cm (8-inch) cake drum, securing it in place with a dab of royal icing. Cut four pieces of dowel to 10 cm (4 inches) in length. Insert the dowels vertically into the centre of the 15-cm (6-inch) tier, keeping them evenly spaced. Place a dab of royal icing on top of each dowel. Place the 13-cm (5-inch) tier on top of the dowels.

STEP 9

Roll out the remaining ivory sugarpaste to 6 mm (⅛ inch) thick. Cut out one oval. Roll up the oval lengthwise to produce a small rosette. Place the rosette in the centre of the 13-cm (5-inch) tier.

STEP 10

Press the remaining ivory sugarpaste into the cameo mould.

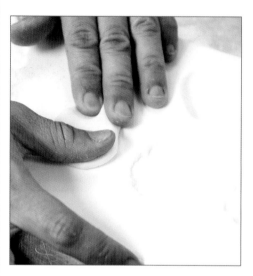

STEP 11

Roll out the leftover lightest salmon-coloured sugarpaste to 6 mm (⅛ inch) thick. Place it on the thin piece of foam and thin the edges with the rounded stick.

STEP 12

Unmould the cameo brooch. Attach it with a little water to the thinned-out oval. Attach the brooch and thinned-out oval to the side of the 13-cm (5-inch) tier.

POLKA DOTS

The height of this sweet and simple cake makes it an eye-catching piece
for a wedding. The ivory dots against the chocolate-brown background
add a playful touch for the modern bride.

TOOLS

- serrated knife
- offset spatula
- 15-cm (6-inch) round cake board
- dough scraper
- 20-cm (8-inch) round cake board
- 25-cm (10-inch) round cake board
- 30-cm (12-inch) round cake board
- rolling pin
- sugarpaste smoother
- pizza cutter
- dowels and shears
- 40-cm (16-inch) round cake drum
- pencil sharpener
- parchment paper
- scissors
- small knife
- small round pastry cutter
- small paintbrush

MATERIALS

- two (15-cm/6-inch) round chocolate cakes (5 cm/ 2 inches high)
- two (20-cm/8-inch) round chocolate cakes (5 cm/ 2 inches high)
- two (25-cm/10-inch) round chocolate cakes (5 cm/ 2 inches high)
- two (30-cm/12-inch) round chocolate cakes (5 cm/ 2 inches high)
- 3.2 kg (7 lb) buttercream
- 3.5 kg (7 ¾ lb) chocolate sugarpaste
- 1.4 kg (3lb 2 oz) white sugarpaste
- gel food colouring – ivory
- cornflour
- royal icing

OVERVIEW

This cake can be completed in one day.

- Make the eight cakes and set aside to cool (approx. 4 hrs)

- Level, split, fill and assemble the tiers (1½ hrs)

- Cover each tier with buttercream (2 hrs, including refrigeration)

- Cover the tiers with sugarpaste and assemble (2 hrs)

- Prepare, make and attach the sugarpaste dots to all the tiers of the cake (approx. 1½ hrs)

two (15-cm/ 6-inch) round chocolate cakes (5 cm/2 inches high)

two (25-cm/ 10-inch) round chocolate cakes (5 cm/2 inches high)

two (20-cm/ 8-inch) round chocolate cakes (5 cm/2 inches hig

two (30-cm/ 12-inch) round chocolate cakes (5 cm/2 inches hig

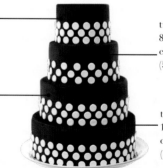

STEP 1

Level the top of each 15-cm (6-inch) round cake and then split them in half horizontally, creating a total of four layers. Fill between each layer with buttercream and stack the four layers on the 15-cm (6-inch) round cake board to create a 10-cm (4-inch) tall tower. Spread a thin coat of buttercream on the top and the sides. Refrigerate for 20 minutes, until it is firm. Spread a thicker coat of buttercream on the top and the sides. Smooth with the bench scraper. Refrigerate for 1 hour, until firm. Repeat these steps for the 20-cm (8-inch), 25-cm (10-inch) and 30-cm (12-inch) rounds. Place each tier on its corresponding cake board.

STEP 2

On a cornflour-covered surface, roll out the chocolate sugarpaste to 3 mm (⅛ inch) thick. Cover each tier and smooth with the sugarpaste smoother. Cut away the excess sugarpaste with the pizza cutter.

STEP 3

Cut the dowels into 10-cm (4-inch) long pieces. Set aside one 30-cm (12-inch) long dowel. Insert four short dowels vertically into the 20-cm (8-inch) tier, six in the 25-cm (10-inch) tier, and eight in the 30-cm (12-inch) tier. Make sure the dowels are evenly spaced and no less than 5 cm (2 inches) from the edge.

STEP 4

Place the 30-cm (12-inch) tier on the cake drum, along with a dab of royal icing to hold it in place. Place a dab of royal icing on top of each dowel. Stack the 25-cm (10-inch) tier on top of the 30-cm (12-inch) tier. Then stack the 20-cm (8-inch) tier on top of the 25-cm (10-inch) tier and end by stacking the 15-cm (6-inch) tier on top of the 20-cm (8-inch) tier. Sharpen a 30-cm (12-inch) long dowel. Drive it vertically through the centre of all four tiers to secure cake together.

STEP 5

Cut a strip of parchment 8-cm (3 inches) wide and long enough to just go around the circumference of the 30-cm (12-inch) tier. Fold the strip in half.

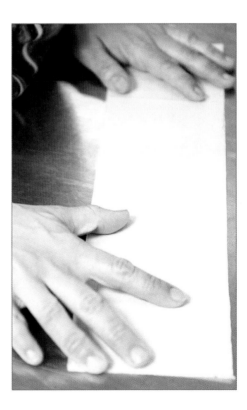

64

STEP 6

Continue folding the strip in half until it is about 5 cm (2 inches) long. Unfold.

STEP 7

Wrap the strip of parchment around the base of the 30-cm (12-inch) tier. The folded creases in the strip will be the guide to where the ivory dots will be placed. Mark these places with a knife along the base of the tier.

STEP 8

Mix the white sugarpaste with the ivory food colouring. Knead it until the colour is uniform. Roll out to 3 mm (⅛ inch) thick. Cut out dots with the small round cutter.

STEP 9

Lightly wet each dot with the paintbrush and attach it to the marked spots on the tier. Continue until you have a row of ivory dots along the bottom of the cake. Roll out the sugarpaste remnants and cut out more dots. Add a second row of dots above the first row. Stagger the second row so the dots are not directly on top of each other. Make sure that the dots are evenly spaced. Continue these steps for a third row of dots. Repeat steps 5 onward for the remaining tiers.

MARDI GRAS

Capture the mystery and flair of Mardi Gras with this two-tiered cake.
The colours can be adjusted for a bolder or more subtle effect.
Your guests will be amazed that even the mask is edible. You will need to
start this cake three days in advance so the mask has enough time to dry.

TOOLS

- clingfilm
- plastic craft mask
- rolling pin
- utility knife
- petal cutters – large and medium
- medium circle cutter
- sugar-craft gun with medium circle attachment
- paintbrush
- 20-cm (8-inch) square cake board
- 30-cm (12-inch) square cake board
- serrated knife
- offset spatula
- dough scraper
- sugarpaste smoother
- pizza cutter
- airbrush and compressor
- 40-cm (16-inch) cake drum
- dowels and clippers
- piping bag and coupler
- #3, #18 and #101 piping tips

MATERIALS

- 4.5 kg (10 lb) white sugarpaste
- gum tragacanth
- cornflour
- gel food colouring – pink, purple, black
- silver luster dust or edible glitter
- vodka
- silver dragées or sugarpaste balls
- two (20-cm/8-inch) square vanilla cakes (5 cm/ 2 inches high)
- two (30-cm/12-inch) square vanilla cakes (5 cm/ 2 inches high)
- 1.5 kg (3 lb) buttercream
- airbrush colour – violet
- royal icing
- black petal dust
- white sweet melts
- feathers

OVERVIEW

This cake will require three days to complete.

DAY ONE
- Prepare the white sugarpaste mask (1 hour)

DAY THREE
- Make the four cakes and set aside to cool (approx. 2 hrs)
- Level, split, fill and assemble the tiers (½ hr)
- Cover each tier with buttercream (1½ hrs including refrigeration)

- Cover the tiers with sugarpaste and assemble (1 hr)
- Pipe the decorations onto the bottom and sides of each tier. Let dry then paint silver (approx. 2 hrs including 1 hr drying time)
- Decorate and attach the sugarpaste mask (approx. 2 hrs)
- Final touches (15 mins)

two (20-cm/ 8-inch) square vanilla cakes (5 cm/2 inches high)

two (30-cm/12-inch) square vanilla cakes (5 cm/2 inches high)

THREE DAYS IN ADVANCE

STEP 1

The mask must be prepared three days in advance to have enough time to dry. Knead 575 grams (20 ounces) of white sugarpaste with ½ teaspoon of gum tragacanth. Mix well and wrap in clingfilm. Set it aside to rest for 15 minutes.

STEP 2

Cover the plastic craft mask with clingfilm. On a surface dusted with cornflour, roll out the prepared white sugarpaste to 6mm (¹/₈ inch) thick. Lay it over the mask and gently press with your fingers while following the contours.

STEP 3

With a utility knife, cut out the eyes and the edges by following the lines of the plastic mask. Allow this to dry for three days.

ASSEMBLING THE CAKE

STEP 4

Dye 850 grams (30 ounces) of the white sugarpaste a deep purple. Roll it out to 6mm (¹/₈ inch) thick. With the large petal cutter, cut out a large petal. Attach it to the centre of the forehead of the sugarpaste mask with a little water.

STEP 6

Using the medium petal cutter, cut out the centre of the purple petal that is attached to the sugarpaste mask.

STEP 5

Cut out a medium circle with the circle cutter. Measure it against the left eye of the mask and trim off a corner of the circle to form a crescent shape. Attach it to the left eye of the sugarpaste mask with a little water.

STEP 7

Dye 280 grams (10 ounces) of the white sugarpaste black. Fill a sugar-craft gun fitted with the medium circle attachment. Squeeze out a long string and attach it with a little water to the sugarpaste mask, following the outlines of the purple sugarpaste pieces. Attach two longer black strings to both sides of the sugarpaste mask.

STEP 8

Using smaller pieces of the black string, create a pattern on the right cheek of the sugarpaste mask and make a black eyebrow for the right eye.

STEP 9

Mix some silver luster dust or edible glitter with vodka. Paint the cut-out petal shape on the forehead of the sugarpaste mask silver. Paint all the other black parts, except for the black eyebrow, silver. Apply silver dragées or sugarpaste silver balls to the cheek design and purple pieces while the silver paint is still wet. Set aside to dry while you prepare the cake tiers.

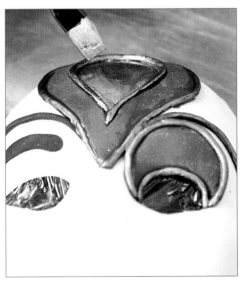

STEP 10

Level the tops of the cakes, split each in half horizontally and fill the 20-cm (8-inch) and 30-cm (12-inch) square tiers, each on its corresponding cake board. Cover each with a thin layer of buttercream. Chill for 20 minutes, then ice the cakes with a thicker coat of buttercream. Smooth with the dough scraper and refrigerate for 1 hour.

STEP 11

Dye 2.8 kg (100 ounces) of the white sugarpaste a medium pink. Roll out to 6 mm (¼ inch) thick and cover the 30-cm (12-inch) square tier. Smooth with the sugarpaste smoother and trim the excess with the pizza cutter. Repeat with the 20-cm (8-inch) square tier.

STEP 12

Fill the airbrush with the violet airbrush colour. Starting with the 30-cm (12-inch) tier, lightly spray the edges of the entire cake to create depth. Repeat with the 20-cm (8-inch) square tier.

STEP 13

Transfer the 30-cm (12-inch) tier to the cake drum, staggering it on the drum so that the corners of the tier are situated at the centre point of each side of the cake drum. Cut eight 10-cm- (4-inch) long dowels. Insert the dowels vertically into the centre of the 30-cm (12-inch) tier, keeping them evenly spaced. Place a dab of royal icing on top of each dowel. Place the 20-cm (8-inch) square tier on top of the 30-cm (12-inch) tier. Stagger it so that the corners of the 20-cm (8-inch) tier are situated at the midpoint of each side of the 30-cm (12-inch) tier.

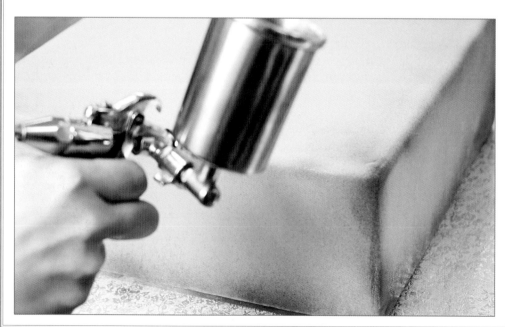

STEP 14

Mix 110 grams (4 oz) of royal icing with the black petal dust to make it light grey. Fill the piping bag with the #3 piping tip and fill the bag with royal icing. Pipe branches onto all eight corners of the two-tiered cake. Change the tip to #101 and pipe leaves on the piped branches. Change the tip to #18 and pipe a border along the base of both tiers. Allow to dry for 1 hour.

STEP 15

Mix some silver luster dust or edible glitter with vodka. With a small paintbrush, carefully paint in all the branches, leaves and piped border. Gently lift the sugarpaste mask from the plastic mask underneath. Place the sugarpaste mask on the cake, with the base of the mask resting on the 30-cm (12-inch) tier and the top resting against one flat side of the 20-cm (8-inch) tier. Secure with some melted white Candy Melts.

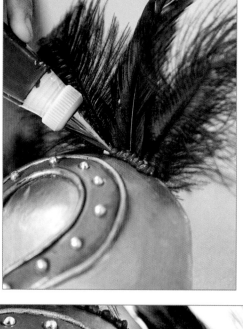

STEP 17

Dye 55 grams (2 fl oz) of royal icing deep purple. Fill a piping bag with the #3 tip, and pipe a border around the edges of the sugarpaste mask.

STEP 16

Attach five feathers to the top of the sugarpaste mask, on the reverse side. Wrap the ends of the remaining feathers with clingfilm. Insert half of the feathers into the top of the 30-cm (12-inch) tier, to the right of the sugarpaste mask. Insert the remaining feathers into the left side of the 30-cm (12-inch) tier.

MOSAIC

The art of creating beautiful designs by assembling small pieces of coloured tiles can be recreated in cake form. The different tones of blue against the stark white cake create a stunning effect.

TOOLS

- 15-cm (6-inch) round cake board
- 25-cm (10-inch) round cake board
- 30-cm (12-inch) round cake board
- serrated knife
- offset spatula
- dough scraper
- clingfilm
- rolling pin
- sugarpaste smoother
- pizza cutter
- dowels and clippers
- pencil sharpener
- blue edible writing pen
- small square cutter
- utility knife
- small paintbrush
- cake stand

MATERIALS

- two (15-cm/6-inch) round vanilla cakes (5 cm/ 2 inches high)
- two (25-cm/10-inch) round vanilla cakes (5 cm/ 2 inches high))
- two (30-cm/12-inch) round vanilla cakes (5 cm/ 2 inches high)
- 15½ cups (2.5 kg) buttercream
- 105 oz. (3 kg) white sugarpaste
- gel food colouring – blue
- cornflour
- royal icing
- clear piping gel

OVERVIEW

Mosaics are very time-consuming designs. The following may take up to two days for a novice to complete. For more elaborate designs, allot yourself enough time to complete.

- Make the six cakes and set aside to cool (approx. 3 hrs)

- Level, split, fill and assemble the tiers (1 hr)

- Cover each tier with buttercream (1½ hrs, including refrigeration)

- Cover the tiers with sugarpaste and assemble (1 hr)

- Draw a design of your choice on the side of the cake (10 mins)

- Cut and attach the sugarpaste tiles (for this design, approx. 2½ hrs)

two (6-inch/ 15-cm) round vanilla cakes (5 cm/2 inches high)

two (10-inch/ 25-cm) round vanilla cakes (5 cm/2 inches high)

two (12-inch/ 30-cm) round vanilla cakes (5 cm/ 2 inches high)

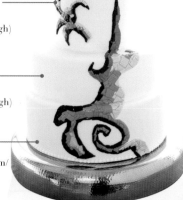

STEP 1

Level the tops of the cakes, split them in half horizontally and fill them with buttercream. Place each on its corresponding cake board to make three tiers, each 4 inches (10 cm) high.

STEP 2

Cover the tiers with a thin layer of buttercream. Chill until firm. Cover with a second coat of buttercream and smooth with a dough scraper. Refrigerate for 1 hour.

STEP 3

Colour 30 grams (1 ounce) of sugarpaste a deep royal blue, 30 grams (1 ounce) a medium sky blue and 30 grams (1 ounce) a light blue. Set aside, covered with clingfilm.

STEP 4

Roll out the remaining white sugarpaste to 6mm (½ inch) thick and cover the 15-cm (6-inch) round tier. Smooth with the sugarpaste smoother and trim excess with the pizza cutter. Repeat with the remaining tiers.

STEP 5

Cut dowels into eighteen 10-cm (4-inch) long pieces. Leave one dowel 12 inches (30 cm) long, but sharpen one end. Insert ten dowels vertically into the 30-cm (12-inch) tier and eight into the 25-cm (10-inch) tier. Space them evenly. Stack the 25-cm (10-inch) tier on top of the 30-cm (12-inch) tier and the 15-cm (6-inch) on top of the 25-cm (10-inch) tier. Drive the 30-cm (12-inch) dowel vertically through the centre of all three tiers. Cover the hole on top with a dab of royal icing.

STEP 6

With the edible ink pen, draw a design of your choice on one side of the cake, from top to bottom.

STEP 7

Roll out the royal blue sugarpaste to 3mm (⅛ inch) thick and then cut out small square tiles with the cutter. Attach the tiles with water to the left-hand side of the design you outlined. Use the utility knife to trim the tiles to follow the curve of the design.

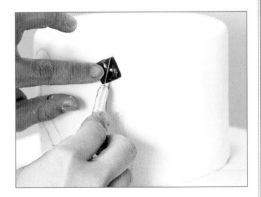

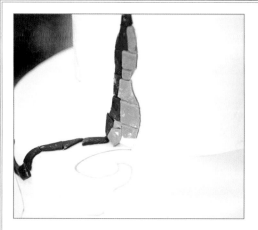

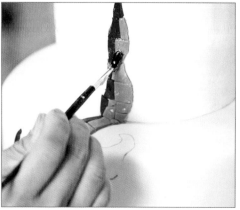

STEP 8

Roll out the sky blue sugarpaste to 3mm (⅛ inch) thick. Cut out square tiles and attach with a little water to the design you outlined, as close as possible to the line of royal blue tiles and leaving space on the right-hand side of the design for the light blue tiles. Trim the tiles with the utility knife as needed to make them fit.

STEP 9

Roll out the light blue sugarpaste to 3mm (⅛ inch) thick. Cut out square tiles and attach with a little water to fill out the design. Trim tiles to make them follow the contour of the design.

STEP 10

Paint over the tiles with clear piping gel to create a glazed tile effect. Put the cake on a cake stand.

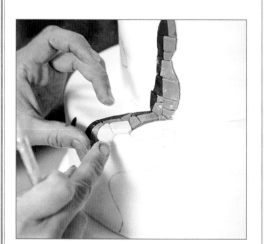

BAROQUE

The damask print has been popular since the early Middle Ages.
The print is becoming popular again and today it can be seen in modern
interior designs and at many weddings.

TOOLS

- large pastry brush
- 40-cm (16-inch) round cake drum
- rolling pin
- sharp knife
- 10-cm (4-inch) square cake board
- 15-cm (6-inch) round cake board
- 20-cm (8-inch) square cake board
- 30-cm (12-inch) round cake board
- 35-cm (14-inch) square cake board
- serrated knife
- offset spatula
- dough scraper
- sugarpaste smoother
- pizza cutter
- clingfilm
- ruler
- quilting tool
- damask stencil
- dowels and shears
- pencil sharpener
- piping bag and coupler
- #18 piping tip
- fuchsia satin ribbon
- glue stick

MATERIALS

- piping gel
- 6 kg (13 lb) white sugarpaste
- cornflour
- two (10-cm/4-inch) square vanilla cakes (5 cm/ 2 inches high)
- two (15-cm/6-inch) round vanilla cakes (5 cm/ 2 inches high)
- two (20-cm/8-inch) square vanilla cakes (5 cm/ 2 inches high)
- two (30-cm/12-inch) round vanilla cakes (5 cm/ 2 inches high)
- two (35-cm/14-inch) square vanilla cakes (5 cm/ 2 inches high)
- 4.5 kg (10 lb) buttercream
- petal dust – black, fuchsia
- royal icing

OVERVIEW

This cake will require two days to complete.

DAY ONE
- Cover the cake drum with sugarpaste

DAY TWO
- Make the ten cakes and set aside to cool (approx. 5 hrs)
- Level, split, fill and assemble the tiers (2 hrs)
- Cover each tier with buttercream (2½ hrs, including refrigeration)
- Cover the tiers with sugarpaste (2 hrs)
- Use the quilting tool to decorate the tiers covered with black sugarpaste (1 hr)
- Apply the stencil to the tiers covered with white sugarpaste (approx. 1 hr; allow 3 hrs for drying)
- Assemble all the tiers (1 hr)
- Final touches (45 mins)

two (10-cm/4-inch) square vanilla cakes (5 cm/2 inches high)

two (15-cm/6-inch) round vanilla cakes (5 cm/2 inches high)

two (20-cm/8-inch) square vanilla cakes (5 cm/2 inches high)

two (30-cm/12-inch) round vanilla cakes (5 cm/2 inches high)

two (35-cm/14-inch) square vanilla cakes (5 cm/2 inches high)

STEP 1

Spread piping gel evenly over the cake drum with the pastry brush. Roll out 275 grams (10 ounces) of the white sugarpaste to 6 mm (¼ inch) thick and cover the cake drum. Trim the excess.

STEP 2

With each cake layer on its corresponding cake board, level the tops of all five tiers, split the cakes in half horizontally and fill between the layers with buttercream. Cover each tier with a thin layer of buttercream and refrigerate for 20 minutes. Cover the top and sides with a thicker coat of buttercream, smooth with the dough scraper and refrigerate for 1 hour.

STEP 3

Dye 4 kg (9 lb) of the white sugarpaste with the black petal dust. Roll out to 6 mm (¼ inch) thick and cover the 10-cm (4-inch), 8-inch (20-cm) and 35-cm (14-inch) square tiers. Smooth with the sugarpaste smoother and trim excess with the pizza cutter. Cover the tiers with clingfilm to prevent the sugarpaste from drying out.

STEP 4

Beginning with the 10-cm (4-inch) tier, place the ruler along the base of the cake and mark it at 2.5-cm (1-inch) intervals with a small knife. Mark it at the same 2.5-cm (1-inch) intervals along the top of the tier. Repeat on all sides.

STEP 5

Holding the ruler vertically, line up the first mark on the bottom with the third mark on the top. Using the quilting tool, make a diagonal line joining these two points. Continue using the ruler and the quilting tool to join the second mark on the bottom to the fourth mark on the top. Continue until there are no more marks on the top. Then, begin joining the first mark on the top with the third mark on the bottom. Repeating this will reveal a quilted diamond pattern. Repeat this procedure on all the square tiers, covered with black sugarpaste.

STEP 6

Roll out the remaining white sugarpaste to 6 mm (¼ inch) thick and cover the 15-cm (6-inch) and 30-cm (12-inch) round tiers. Smooth with the sugarpaste smoother and trim the excess with the pizza cutter.

STEP 7

Dye 110 grams (4 oz) of royal icing with black petal dust. Hold the damask stencil against the side of the 6-inch (15-cm) round tier (you may need someone to help you hold it steady).

STEP 8

Using a small offset spatula, spread a thin layer of black royal icing on the stencil. Scrape off the excess.

STEP 9

Gently lift off the stencil, without smudging the design. Repeat this procedure until the entire side of the cake is covered with the damask print. Do the same for the 30-cm (12-inch) round tier. Allow to dry for three hours.

STEP 10

Cut the dowels into 26 10-cm (4-inch) long pieces. Insert eight vertically into the 35-cm (14-inch) tier, eight into the 30-cm (12-inch) tier, six into the 20-cm (8-inch) tier and four into the 15-cm (6-inch) tier. Space the dowels evenly and leave a space of 5-cm (2 inches) from the edge. Transfer the 35-cm (14-inch) tier to the cake drum, securing it with a dab of royal icing. Place a dab of royal icing on the top of the dowels and begin stacking the tiers: the 12-inch (30-cm) tier on top of the 35-cm (14-inch) tier, the 20-cm (8-inch) on the 30-cm (12-inch), the 15-cm (6-inch) on the 20-cm (8-inch) and the 10-cm (4-inch) tier on the 15-cm (6-inch). Sharpen one end of a 30-cm (12-inch) long dowel. Drive it vertically through the centre of the tiers. Cover the hole on top of the 10-cm (4-inch) tier with some royal icing.

STEP 11
Dye 110 grams (4 oz) of royal icing with fuchsia petal dust. Fill the piping bag and, using the #18 piping tip, pipe a border along the bottom of all five tiers.

STEP 12
Attach the fuchsia ribbon to the cake drum with the glue stick. Tie a small bow and attach the bow to the front of the cake drum with more glue.

BABY SHOWER

The birth of a baby is always a special occasion. Celebrate with this cute design. Change the colours, if you want, for a baby girl shower. Start this cake at least a day in advance to let the sugarpaste decorations dry.

TOOLS

- pastry brush
- 35-cm (14-inch) square cake drum
- rolling pin
- sharp knife
- serrated knife
- offset spatula
- 13-cm (5-inch) square cake board
- 18-cm (7-inch) square cake board
- 20-cm (8-inch) square cake board
- 23-cm (9-inch) square cake board
- dough scraper
- sugarpaste smoother
- pizza cutter
- clingfilm
- sugarpaste ribbon cutter
- paintbrush
- small circle cutter
- scissors
- ruler
- small blossom cutter
- #12 piping tip
- small sharp knife
- dowels and shears
- pencil sharpener
- piping bag and coupler
- scalloped cutters – large and medium
- blue satin ribbon
- glue stick

MATERIALS

- piping gel
- 4.5 kg (10 lb) ivory sugarpaste
- cornflour
- two (13-cm/ 5-inch) square vanilla cakes (5 cm/ 2 inches high)
- two (7-inch/18 cm) square vanilla cakes (5 cm/ 2 inches high)
- two (20-cm/8-inch) square vanilla cakes (5 cm/ 2 inches high)
- two (23-cm/ 9-inch) square vanilla cakes (5 cm/ 2 inches high)
- 2 kg (4¼ lb) buttercream
- gel food colouring – green, blue
- royal icing

OVERVIEW

This cake will require two days to complete.

DAY ONE
- Cover cake drum with sugarpaste (15 mins)
- Prepare sugarpaste bows (1½ hrs)

DAY TWO
- Make the eight cakes and set aside to cool (approx. 4 hrs)

- Level, split, fill and assemble the tiers (2 hrs)
- Cover each tier with buttercream (2½ hrs, including refrigeration)
- Cover the tiers with sugarpaste (2 hrs)
- Decorate each tier (2½ hrs)
- Assemble all the tiers (1 hr)
- Final touches (½ hr)

two (13-cm/ 5-inch) square vanilla cakes (5 cm/2inches high)

two (18-cm/ 7-inch) square vanilla cakes (5 cm/2 inches high)

two (20-cm/8-inch) square vanilla cakes (5 cm/2inches high)

two (23-cm/ 9-inch) square vanilla cakes (5 cm/2inches high)

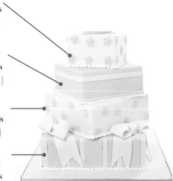

STEP 1

With the pastry brush, spread piping gel over the 35-cm (14-inch) cake drum. On a cornflour-covered work surface, roll out 275 grams (10 ounces) of ivory sugarpaste to 6 mm (¼ inch) thick. Cover the cake drum and trim off the excess with the sharp knife.

STEP 2

Level the tops of all the cakes with the serrated knife. Split them in half horizontally. Place each cake on its corresponding cake board and fill all four layers with buttercream. Cover the tiers with a thin layer of buttercream. Chill until firm. Cover with a second coat of buttercream and smooth with the dough scraper. Refrigerate for 1 hour.

STEP 3

Dye 2.3 kg (80 ounces) of sugarpaste pastel blue and 110 grams (4 ounces) pastel green. Roll out the remaining ivory sugarpaste to 6 mm (¼ inch) thick and cover the 13-cm (5-inch) tier. Smooth with the sugarpaste smoother. Trim off excess. Save trimmings, and wrap in clingfilm. Repeat with the 20-cm (8-inch) tier.

STEP 4

Roll out the blue sugarpaste to 6 mm (¼ inch) thick and cover the 18-cm (7-inch) tier. Smooth with the sugarpaste smoother. Trim off excess and save trimmings, wrapping them in clingfilm. Repeat with the 23-cm (9-inch) tier.

STEP 5

Transfer the 23-cm (9-inch) tier to the prepared cake drum. Roll out the green sugarpaste to 3 mm (⅛ inch) thick. With the sugarpaste ribbon cutter, cut out strips, each 4 cm (1½ inches) wide. Roll up the strips to keep them from drying out while you work. Starting 6 mm (¼ inch) from the edge, attach three green strips vertically on each side of the tier. Space them evenly on each side.

STEP 6

Now roll out the reserved ivory sugarpaste to 3 mm (⅛ inch) thick and cut out 6 mm (¼ inch) wide strips. Using a wet paintbrush, attach these along both sides of each green strip. Trim off the excess sugarpaste along the top of the tier.

STEP 7

Roll out the reserved blue and green sugarpastes to 3 mm (⅛ inch) thick. With the small circle cutter, cut out small round dots from each sugarpaste colour. Attach the dots to the sides of the ivory-coloured 20-cm (8-inch) tier, alternating the colours.

STEP 8

Now decorate the 18-cm (7-inch) tier. Roll out the rest of the green sugarpaste to 3 mm (⅛ inch) thick. Cut out four strips, 1 cm (½ inch) wide and 23 cm (9 inches) long. Attach a strip along the bottom edge of each side of the 18-cm (7-inch) tier. Pinch together where the strips meet at the corners and cut off the excess with scissors.

STEP 9

With the ruler, mark a line 5 cm (2 inches) from the top of the tier. Roll out ivory sugarpaste to 6 mm (¼ inch) thick. Cut four strips that are 1 cm (½ inch) wide and 23 cm (9 inches) long. Attach them to the marked line on the cake. Pinch together where the strips meet at the corners and cut with scissors.

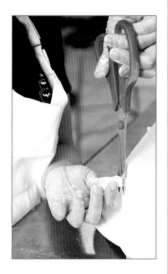

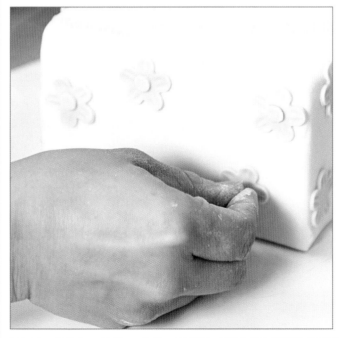

STEP 10

To decorate the 13-cm (5-inch) tier, roll out the remaining blue sugarpaste to 3 mm (⅛ inch) thick. Cut out flowers with the blossom cutter. Attach the flowers to the 13-cm (5-inch) tier. Roll out green sugarpaste to 3 mm (⅛ inch) thick and cut out dots with the #12 tip. Attach the dots to the centre of each flower.

STEP 11

Tear off pieces of clingfilm and roll them into balls.

STEP 12

Roll out the remaining ivory sugarpaste to 3 mm (⅛ inch) thick. Cut out four strips that are 5 cm (2 inches) wide and 20 cm (8 inches) long. Cut four more strips, 5 cm (2 inches) wide and 8 cm (3 inches) long. Wet the centre of one 20-cm (8-inch) long strip. Place a piece of balled-up clingfilm on each side of the wet spot.

STEP 13

Bring both ends of the strip toward the wet centre of the strip. Pinch together.

STEP 14

Wet a 8-cm (3-inch) strip and wrap it around the centre of the bow. Set aside to dry overnight. Repeat with the other strips, making a total of four bows.

STEP 15

Cut twenty 10-cm (4-inch) long dowels and one 30-cm (12-inch) long dowel. Sharpen one end of the 30-cm (12-inch) dowel. Insert eight dowels vertically into the 23-cm (9-inch) tier, six into the 20-cm (8-inch) tier, and six into the 18-cm (7-inch) tier. Stack one tier on top of the other, placing the 23-cm (9-inch) tier on the bottom, then the 20-cm (8-inch) tier, the 18-cm (7-inch) tier, and ending with the 13-cm (5-inch) tier. Turn the tiers so they are staggered, instead of having the edges parallel to each other. This will leave the corners of the 23-cm (9-inch) tier open for the bows. Insert the 30-cm (12-inch) long dowel through the centre of the tiers. Pipe white beads of royal icing along the base of each tier.

STEP 16

Roll out blue sugarpaste to 3 mm (⅛ inch) thick. Cut out a scalloped circle with the large scalloped cutter. Attach with a little water to the top of the 13-cm (5-inch) tier. Roll out the green sugarpaste and cut out a circle with the medium scalloped cutter. Moisten and attach to the centre of the blue circle.

STEP 17

On each corner of the 23-cm (9-inch) tier, attach a strip of ivory sugarpaste that is 5 cm (2 inches) wide and 15 cm (6 inches) long. Cut out a 'V' shape from each end. With royal icing, attach the sugarpaste bows on each strip. Remove the clingfilm. Attach the satin ribbon to the cake drum with the glue stick.

TOPSY-TURVY

Who can resist the look of a whimsical cake? The silver and gold colours complement each other and contrast beautifully with the black background – all topped with a golden crown. The crown will need to dry overnight, so plan ahead.

TOOLS

- serrated knives – large and small
- offset spatula
- 30-cm (12-inch) round cake board
- 15-cm (6-inch) round cake board
- dough scraper
- rolling pin
- sugarpaste smoother
- pizza cutter
- small sharp knife
- clingfilm
- medium quilting tool
- paintbrushes
- painter's palette
- sugarpaste ribbon cutter
- heart-shaped cutter
- 10-cm (4-inch) round tin
- scissors
- cake stand

MATERIALS

- two (20-cm/8-inch) round vanilla cakes (5 cm/ 2 inches high)
- 550 grams (1 lb 3 oz) buttercream
- 850 grams (1¾ lb) white sugarpaste
- gel food colouring – black, golden yellow
- cornflour
- luster dust or edible glitter – gold, silver
- vodka
- black Candy Melts

OVERVIEW

This cake will require two days to complete.

DAY ONE
- Prepare and make the yellow sugarpaste crown (1 hr)

DAY TWO
- Make the two cakes and set aside to cool (approx. 1 hr)

- Level, split, fill and assemble the two tiers (½ hr)

- Cut and shape the cake (approx. 1 hr)

- Cover the cake with buttercream (1½ hrs, including refrigeration)

- Cover the cake with sugarpaste (1 hr)

- Decorate the cake with the quilting tool (½ hr)

- Cut out and attach the diamond sugarpaste pieces and balls (1 hr)

- Final touches (1 hr)

two (20-cm/8-inch) round vanilla cakes (5 cm/2 inches high)

STEP 1

With the large serrated knife, level the cake layers, split them in half horizontally and fill with buttercream. With the cake on the 30-cm (12-inch) cake board, refrigerate for 1 hour to firm up the crumb. Spread a dab of buttercream on the top of the cake and place the 15-cm (6-inch) cake board in the centre. This will become the bottom of the cake.

STEP 2

With a small serrated knife, carve around the top edge of the cake, using the 15-cm (6-inch) board as the guide.

STEP 3

With a downward motion, cut the cake from the 15-cm (6-inch) diameter on top to the 20-cm (8-inch) diameter on the bottom. This will give the cake tapered sides.

STEP 4

Flip the cake upside down and, holding the large serrated knife at a 45-degree angle against the side of the cake, cut straight across to cut a wedge off the top.

STEP 5

Spread a little buttercream on the top of the cake that remains. Turn the wedge 180 degrees and place it back on the top of the cake. Now the cake will have a tapered top and tapered sides.

STEP 6

Spread a thin coat of buttercream on the top and sides of the cake. Refrigerate until firm. Cover the top and sides with a thicker coat of buttercream. Smooth with a dough scraper and refrigerate for 1 hour. Colour 675 grams (24 ounces) of sugarpaste black. Roll out to 6 mm (¼ inch) thick and cover the cake.

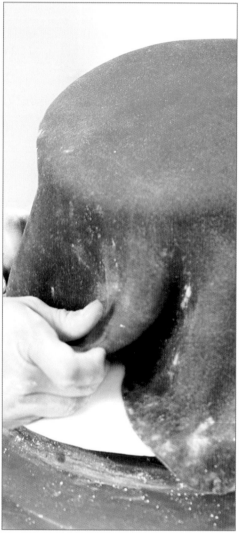

STEP 7

Smooth with the sugarpaste smoother and trim off excess with the pizza cutter. Save the excess black sugarpaste and cover it with clingfilm. Press the quilting tool into the sides of the cake. The markings will act as a guide to where the gold and silver diamonds will be placed.

STEP 9

Wet each diamond with a little water and attach them to the side of the cake. Vertically, alternate between yellow and grey. Leave the next row of diamonds black. Then, repeat with the yellow and grey diamonds. Some may need to be cut.

STEP 8

Dye 55 grams (2 ounces) of sugarpaste grey and 110 grams (4 ounces) golden yellow. Roll out the grey sugarpaste to 3 mm (⅛ inch) thick. With the quilting tool, cut out diamond shapes. Repeat with the yellow sugarpaste. Save the excess sugarpaste, wrapped in clingfilm.

STEP 10

Roll out ½-teaspoon balls with the left-over yellow and grey sugarpaste. Roll out ¼- teaspoon balls with the black sugarpaste. Attach the balls to the base of the cake with a little water, alternating the colours.

STEP 11

Mix the gold luster dust or edible glitter with vodka on the painter's palette. Do the same with the silver luster dust or edible glitter. With a small paintbrush, paint the yellow diamonds and balls gold. Then, paint the grey diamonds and balls silver.

STEP 12

Roll out the remaining yellow sugarpaste to 6 mm (¼ inch) thick. With the sugarpaste ribbon cutter, cut out a strip that is 13 cm (5 inches) wide and 40 cm (15 inches) long. Using the bottom half of a heart-shaped cutter, cut pieces from one long side of the strip to make pointy ends. Wrap this strip around a 10-cm (4-inch) round tin. Cut the excess with scissors and pinch the ends together. This will be the crown. Allow to dry overnight. When it has dried, remove the tin. Paint the crown gold with the paintbrush. Roll out six ¼-teaspoon balls of grey sugarpaste. Attach to each of the pointed ends of the crown and paint silver. Attach the crown to the cake with some melted black candy melts. Transfer the cake to the round cake stand.

FANCY CUSHION

The look of your favourite cushion can be easily replicated in a cake.
The gilded buttons and tassels make it extra fancy.

TOOLS

- 35-cm (14-inch) square cake board
- serrated knife
- offset spatula
- dough scraper
- rolling pin
- sugarpaste smoother
- clingfilm
- pizza cutter
- small sharp knife
- dog bone tool
- veining tool
- measuring spoons
- floral mould
- clay gun with rope attachment
- utility knife
- paintbrushes
- clothing steamer
- cake stand

MATERIALS

- one (20-cm/8-inch) square chocolate cake (8 cm/ 3 inches high)
- 500 grams (1 lb 3 oz) buttercream
- 1 kg (1 lb 3 oz) white sugarpaste
- gel food colouring – red, lemon yellow, leaf green
- cornflour
- royal icing
- brown petal dust
- luster dust or edible glitter – gold
- vodka

OVERVIEW

This cake will require two days to complete.

DAY ONE
- Make the cake and set aside to cool (approx. 1 hr)

- Level, split, fill and assemble (1 hr)

  You can split and fill the cake on day one and then put it in the freezer. Freezing the cake will make it easier to carve.

DAY TWO
- Cut and shape the cake (approx. 1 hr)

- Cover with buttercream (1½ hrs including refrigeration)

- Cover with sugarpaste (1 hr)

- Make and decorate the top of the cushion with the sugarpaste buttons (1 hr)

- Prepare and attach the sugarpaste rope and tassels (1 hr)

- Final touches (½ hr)

one (20-cm/8-inch) round chocolate cake (8-cm/3 inches) high

STEP 1

On the 35-cm (14-inch) board, level the top of the 20-cm (8-inch) square cake with the serrated knife. Split horizontally into three layers. Fill between the layers with buttercream and chill for 1 hour, or freeze overnight, to firm up the crumb.

STEP 2

With the serrated knife, round out the edges of the cake, carving until the edges are more sloped down on the top and the middle is more raised, to simulate a cushion. Cover lightly with buttercream. Chill until firm. Cover with a second coat of buttercream and smooth with the dough scraper. Refrigerate for 1 hour.

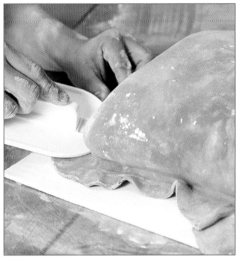

STEP 3

Dye 950 grams (1 lb 1 oz) of white sugarpaste with red, yellow and a touch of green food colouring to achieve a burnt orange colour. On a cornflour-covered surface, roll sugarpaste out to 6 mm (¼ inch) thick and cover the cushion. Smooth with the sugarpaste smoother and trim off the excess.

STEP 4

Using the sharp knife, push in the sugarpaste at the base of the cake.

STEP 5
Use the dog bone tool to make a dent in the places where the buttons will sit.

STEP 6
With the veining tool, mark lines around the dents to imitate the puckering of fabric.

STEP 7
Dye the remaining 55 grams (2 ounces) of white sugarpaste a golden yellow. Roll out ¼-teaspoon balls. Press the balls into the floral mould to flatten and add texture creating button shapes. Glue each button with a dab of royal icing onto the dented spots on the cushion.

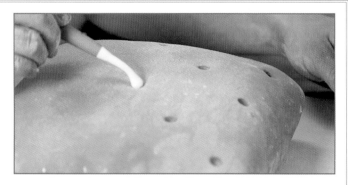

STEP 8

Fill the clay gun with yellow sugarpaste. Squeeze out a long string. Twist the string of sugarpaste to achieve a rope effect. Attach to the cushion with a little water.

STEP 9

Roll out a little of the remaining yellow sugarpaste to 1.5 mm (1/16 inch) thick. Use the utility knife to cut small slits into the sugarpaste.

STEP 10

Moisten the uncut portion of the piece of sugarpaste and roll it up. Make four of these 'tassels' and attach them to the corners of the cushion with a little water. Roll out four ¼-teaspoon balls and attach to the top of the tassel to make the knot of the tassel.

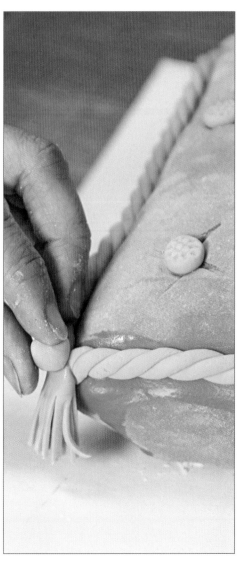

STEP 11

Apply brown petal dust with a paintbrush to the 'puckered' lines around the buttons of the cushion. Then, mix the gold luster dust or edible glitter with vodka and paint the rope, tassels and buttons of the cushion gold.

STEP 12

With the clothing steamer, steam the entire cake to remove the cornflour. Transfer the cake to a cake stand.

ROSE BOUQUET

Gumpaste flowers can be quite time consuming to make, especially for the novice. Starting one week in advance is always a good idea. But when your guests are stunned by the lifelike beauty of this bouquet, it will all seem worth it.

TOOLS

- pastry brush
- 25-cm (10-inch) round cake drum
- small rolling pin
- small palette knife
- cocktail sticks
- polystyrene block
- small, medium and large rose cutters
- piece of thin foam
- utility knife
- rounded stick
- calyx cutter
- serrated knife
- offset spatula
- dough scraper
- pizza cutter
- sugar-craft gun with large circle disk
- small paintbrush
- red and white satin ribbons, 2-cm (¾ inch) wide
- glue stick

MATERIALS

- 2.5 kg (5 ½lb) sugarpaste
- gel food colouring – red, leaf green, brown, lemon yellow, ivory
- piping gel
- vodka
- 510 g (1 lb 2 oz) gumpaste
- shortening
- two (15-cm/6-inch) round chocolate cakes (8-cm/ 3 inches high)
- 650 g (1½ lb) buttercream
- cornflour
- royal icing

OVERVIEW

Gumpaste flowers can be very labour intensive. In order to complete enough roses to cover the entire cake, we recommend that the roses be made over the period of one week.

DAY ONE
- Prepare the cake drum and cover with sugarpaste (15 mins)

DAY TWO
- Prepare and make the two cakes and set aside to cool (approx. 1 hr)

- Level, split, fill and assemble each tier (1 hr)

- Cover with buttercream (1½ hrs including refrigeration)

- Cover cake with sugarpaste (½ hr)

- Prepare and attach the sugarpaste stems (1 hr)

- Attach the previously prepared sugarpaste roses (1½ hrs)

two (15-cm/6-inch) round chocolate cakes (3 inches/8-cm high)

STEP 1

Divide 510 grams (18 ounces) of sugarpaste into three balls. Colour the balls dark brown, medium brown and light brown. Roll each ball into a sausage shape. Twist the three colours together and mix them just enough to achieve a marbled effect.

STEP 2

With the pastry brush, brush the piping gel onto the cake drum with the piping gel. With the rolling pin, roll out the marbled brown sugarpaste and cover the cake drum. Using a small palette knife, score the sugarpaste to get a woodgrain effect. Dilute the ivory gel colour with some vodka and brush it over the sugarpaste-covered cake drum to stain it.

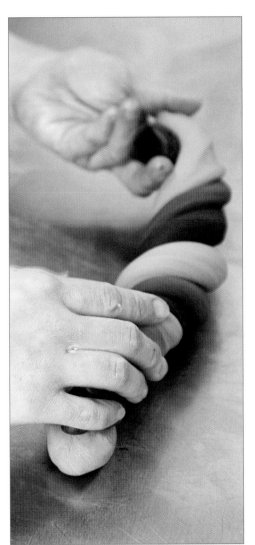

STEP 3

Colour 450 grams (16 ounces) of the gumpaste a deep red and colour 55 grams (2 ounces) green. Break off pieces of the red gumpaste to roll into 1-cm, 6-mm and 3-mm (½-, ¼- and ⅛-inch) balls. You will need a total of 60 balls. Roll each ball into a teardrop shape. Stick a cocktail stick into the wide end of each teardrop shape and then stick them upright into the polystyrene. Allow to dry overnight.

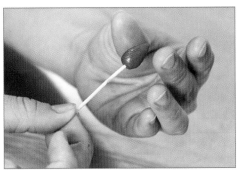

STEP 4

The next day, with the rolling pin, roll out the remaining red gumpaste as thinly as possible on a surface greased with shortening. Cut out four sets of petals with the large rose cutter. Place one set on the thin foam and cover the other three sets with clingfilm. Using the utility knife, cut out one petal from the first set. Using the rounded stick like a rolling pin, thin the petal on one side.

STEP 5

Lightly moisten the thick side of the petal and wrap it around the teardrop cone with the thin side up. Discard the other petals on the set.

STEP 6

Take the second set of petals. With the rounded stick, thin out the edges of all the petals on the thin foam. Make incisions with the utility knife to separate the petals a little.

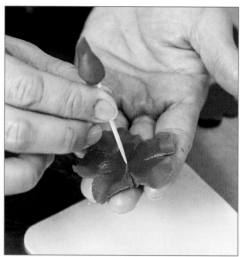

STEP 7

Wet the centre of the petal set and insert the cocktail stick with the teardrop cone into the centre. Move the petals up the cocktail stick until the petals reach the base of the cone.

Attach the petals to the cone one by one, alternating with the petals that are opposite each other.

STEP 9

Repeat with the remaining two sets of petals until you have a full rose. Furl the petals gently with your fingers to get a natural look.

STEP 10

Roll out the green gumpaste thinly. Cut it with the calyx cutter. Using the rounded stick, elongate the points on the thin foam. Wet the centre with a little water and attach to the base of the rose. Stand the rose back in the polystyrene to dry. Repeat all the steps with the small, medium and large roses. You will need at least 60 roses to cover the cake.

ASSEMBLING THE BOUQUET

STEP 11

Level the top of one of the cake layers with a serrated knife and leave the second layer with a rounded top. Split both layers in half horizontally with the serrated knife. Stack the layers, starting with the levelled layer and ending with the rounded top of the second layer on top. Fill between each layer with 40 grams (1½ oz) of buttercream, spread with the offset spatula. Cover the top and sides of the cake tower with a thin, smooth coating of buttercream. Refrigerate until firm, then apply a second coat of buttercream and smooth with a dough scraper. Refrigerate for 1 hour until firm.

STEP 12

Colour 1.5 kg (52 ounces) of the sugarpaste dark green. With the yellow and green gel colours, dye 510 grams (18 ounces) of the sugarpaste a light green.

STEP 13

Roll out 800 grams (28 ounces) of the dark green to 6 mm (¼ inch) thick on a surface dusted with cornflour. Cover the prepared cake with it and trim off the excess with the pizza cutter. Save the trimmings and cover with clingfilm. Transfer the covered cake to the cake drum. Secure with a dab of royal icing.

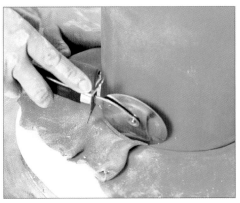

STEP 14

Soften the dark green and light green sugarpaste with shortening. Using the sugar-craft gun with the circle disk, squeeze out 10 cm- (4 inch) long rose stems with the dark green and light green. You will need about 50 stems of each colour to cover the cake. With a paintbrush and water, moisten each stem and attach it to the side of the cake. Alternate between the two shades of green. You may need to trim the tops with a utility knife to keep all the stems even.

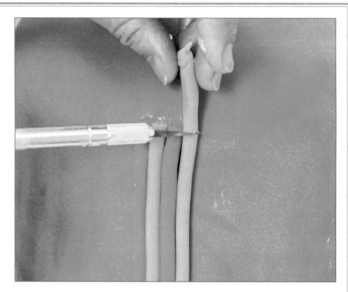

STEP 15

Begin attaching the dried roses to the top of the cake with green-coloured royal icing. Start with the large roses and fill any gaps with the medium and small roses.

STEP 16

Use the glue stick to attach the red satin ribbon to the cake drum. Tie the white satin ribbon around the middle of the bouquet.

LUSTROUS PEACOCK

Capturing the beauty of a peacock, this three-tiered cake makes a stunning centrepiece for any celebration. Note the delicacy of each feather and edible brooch. Give yourself a week to make this cake.

TOOLS

- 35-cm (14-inch) round cake drum
- pastry brush
- rolling pin
- sugarpaste ribbon cutter
- paintbrushes – small and large
- parchment paper
- baking tray
- small and large oval cutters
- two piping bags and couplers
- #2 piping tip
- pizza cutter
- utility knife
- flower formers
- 10-cm (4-inch) round tin
- 15-cm (6-inch) round tin
- 30-cm (12-inch) square cake drum
- painter's palette
- 15-cm (6-inch) round cake board
- pencil
- scissors
- 23-cm (9-inch) petal-shaped tin
- 25-cm (10-inch) round cake board
- 30-cm (12-inch) round cake board
- serrated knife
- offset spatula
- dough scraper
- sugarpaste smoother
- 14 wooden dowels (4 inches/10-cm long)
- one 30-cm (12-inch) long dowel and pencil sharpener
- 2-cm- (¾-inch) wide purple grosgrain ribbon
- glue stick

MATERIALS

- two (15-cm/6-inch) round vanilla cakes (5 cm/2 inches high)
- two (23-cm/9-inch) petal-shaped vanilla cakes (5 cm/2 inches high)
- two (30-cm/12-inch) round vanilla cakes (5 cm/2 inches high)
- 3.8 kg (8½ lb) sugarpaste
- gel food colouring – sky blue, violet, black
- 280 g (10 oz) gumpaste
- piping gel
- cornflour
- luster dust or edible glitter – midnight blue, peacock blue, silver, pearl, deep rose, Aztec gold
- royal icing
- fine silver dragées or sugarpaste beads
- shortening
- vodka
- black petal dust
- pearl dragées or sugarpaste beads
- 2.4 kg (5¼ lb) buttercream

OVERVIEW

This cake will require preparations one week in advance.

ONE WEEK AHEAD
- Cover the cake drum (15 mins)
- Make the 12 bow loops (1½ hrs)
- Prepare the sugarpaste brooch (1 hr)
- Prepare the hearts and scrolls (2 hrs)
- Make the black sugarpaste feathers (1½ hrs)

THREE DAYS AHEAD
- Paint all the hearts, scrolls and ovals with gold paint (1 hr)

- Final touches to the sugarpaste feathers (1 hr)
- Assemble the bows (1 hr)

FINAL DAY
- Make the six cakes and set aside to cool (approx. 3 hrs)
- Level, split, fill and assemble the tiers (2 hrs)
- Cover each tier with buttercream (2½ hrs including refrigeration)
- Cover the tiers with sugarpaste (2 hrs)

two (15-cm/6-inch) round vanilla cakes (5 cm/2 inches high)

two (23-cm/9-inch) petal-shaped vanilla cakes (5 cm/2 inches high)

two (30-cm/12-inch) round vanilla cakes (5 cm/2 inches high)

ONE WEEK AHEAD

STEP 1

Colour 3 kg (105 ounces) sugarpaste sky blue and 700 grams (25 ounces) light violet. Colour the gumpaste black.

STEP 2

Brush the 35-cm (14-inch) round cake drum with piping gel. On a cornflour-dusted surface, roll out the violet sugarpaste 6 mm (¼ inch) thick and cover the cake drum.

STEP 3

Roll out the remaining violet sugarpaste to 6 mm (¼ inch) thick. With the ribbon cutter, cut out 12 strips 5 cm (2 inches) wide and 10 cm (4 inches) long. Flip one strip over. Moisten the outer edge of each strip on both sides. Fold over about 6-mm (¼ inch) on each side so that the strip is now 4 cm (1½ inches) wide.

STEP 4

Place some rolled up plastic in the centre and pinch both ends together. Repeat with the remaining strips to get 12 bow loops. (Remove plastic when dry).

STEP 5

With a small paintbrush, dust the centre of each bow loop with the rose luster dust or edible glitter. Place on parchment paper to dry.

STEP 6

Roll out 55 grams (2 ounces) of white sugarpaste. With the oval cutters, cut out three large ovals and one small oval. Spread each with a little royal icing thinned with water, then cover each with fine silver dragées or sugarpaste beads. Set aside to dry.

STEP 7

Fill a piping bag with royal icing and attach the #2 piping tip. Pipe small hearts and curled scrolls about 1.5 cm (⅔ inch) in size onto parchment paper. You will need enough to cover the base of all three tiers. Make extras in case of breakage. Set aside to dry.

STEP 8

Roll out the black gumpaste as thinly as possible on a surface greased with shortening. Using the pizza cutter, cut out feather shapes.

STEP 9

Cut fine slits into both sides of the feather with a sharp utility knife. You will need seven feathers and a few extras in case of breakage. Place on flower formers to dry.

THREE DAYS AHEAD

STEP 10

Using a 10-cm (4-inch) round tin and a 15-cm (6-inch) round tin, trace and cut out circles from the 30-cm (12-inch) square cake drum. Brush both with piping gel and cover them with the sky blue sugarpaste. These will be the separators for the tiers.

STEP 11

Make gold paint by mixing gold luster dust or edible glitter and vodka. Paint all the hearts, scrolls and ovals gold. Let dry. Attach scrolls to ovals using royal icing to form a gold brooch.

STEP 12
Gently dust the feathers with black petal dust.

STEP 13
Tint a small amount of royal icing black and pipe a line lengthwise down each feather with the #2 piping tip. Let dry.

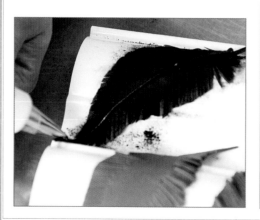

STEP 14
Roll three 6 mm (¼ inch) balls of violet sugarpaste. Gently push four bow loops into each ball to form a bow. Place a dab of royal icing in the centre and attach a large gold brooch to cover the sugarpaste-ball centre. Adorn each brooch with a few pearl dragées or sugarpaste beads.

ASSEMBLING THE CAKE

STEP 15

Level the tops of the cake layers. Split the 15-cm (6-inch) round layers in half horizontally and fill between the layers with buttercream. Set the tier on the 15-cm (6-inch) round cake board to make a 10-cm- (4-inch) high cake tower.

STEP 16

Using the 23-cm (9-inch) petal tin, trace and cut out a 23-cm (9-inch) petal-shaped cake board from the 25-cm (10-inch) round cake board. Split, fill and stack the petal-shaped cake layers on this board.

STEP 17

Split, fill and stack the 30-cm (12-inch) cake layers on the 30-cm (12-inch) round cake board. Cover the cake tiers with buttercream and smooth with the dough scraper. Refrigerate until firm. Cover with a second coat of buttercream and smooth with the dough scraper. Refrigerate for 1 hour.

STEP 18

Roll out the sky blue sugarpaste to 6 mm (¼ inch) thick. Cover all three tiers and smooth with the sugarpaste smoother. Trim excess sugarpaste with the pizza cutter.

STEP 19

Transfer the 30-cm (12-inch) round cake to the decorated 35-cm (14-inch) cake drum. Secure with a dab of royal icing. Place the 15-cm (6-inch) separator in the centre of this tier. Gently trace around the edges of the separator with a knife so you can see where to place the dowels. Remove the separator and insert eight dowels evenly into the area where you have scored. Apply small dabs of royal icing to the tops of each dowel. Place the 15-cm (6-inch) separator. Squeeze a dab of royal icing onto the separator. Stack the petal-shaped tier

onto the separator. Place the 10-cm (4-inch) separator onto the centre of this tier. Score gently, remove and insert the remaining six dowels evenly. Place dabs of royal icing on the tops of each dowel. Replace the 10-cm (4-inch) separator. Apply a dab of royal icing and place the top tier onto the cake.

STEP 20

Sharpen one end of the 30-cm (12-inch) dowel with the pencil sharpener. Drive the dowel, sharp end down, through the three tiers and the separators. Cover the hole with a dab of royal icing.

STEP 21

With a paintbrush, apply midnight blue luster dust or edible glitter into the grooves of the petal-shaped tier. Dust peacock blue luster dust on the edges of all three tiers. With the large paintbrush, dust the tiers with silver and pearl dust.

STEP 22

With small dabs of royal icing, attach the gold hearts along the base of the three tiers. The hearts should be pointing down on the top two tiers and pointing up on the bottom tier.

STEP 23

Randomly attach the violet bows with royal icing, one per tier. Surround each bow with black feathers. Secure with royal icing. Cover the hole on the top tier with the remaining small gold brooch. Attach random pearl dragées or sugarpaste beads to the three tiers. With the glue stick, attach the purple ribbon to the cake drum.

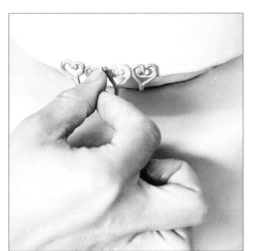

URBAN SAFARI

Bring the look of the jungle to your city life. The unusual shape of the four tiers makes this cake very unique. By mixing round and square tiers and different prints, this is not your typical wedding cake.

TOOLS

- serrated knife
- offset spatula
- 10-cm (4-inch) square cake board
- dough scraper
- 25-cm (10-inch) square cake board
- 5-cm (2-inch) round cake board
- 10-cm (4-inch) round cake board
- scissors
- 15-cm (6-inch) round cake board
- 30-cm (12-inch) square cake board
- rolling pin
- sugarpaste smoother
- pizza cutter
- small sharp knife
- dowels and shears
- pencil sharpener
- veining tool
- paintbrush
- painter's palette
- piping bag and coupler
- #12 piping tip
- 40-cm (16-inch) cake drum

MATERIALS

- two (10-cm/4-inch) round vanilla cakes (5 cm/ 2 inches high)
- two (15-cm/6-inch) square vanilla cakes (5 cm/ 2 inches high)
- two (20-cm/8-inch) round vanilla cakes (5 cm/ 2 inches high)
- two (30-cm/12-inch) square vanilla cakes (5 cm/ 2 inches high)
- 2.3 kg (5 lb) buttercream
- 3.8 kg (8 lb 6 oz) white sugarpaste
- cornflour
- gel food colouring – black, brown
- vodka
- royal icing

OVERVIEW

This cake will require two days to complete.

DAY ONE
- The cake can be split, filled and kept frozen one day in advance for ease of carving.
- Make the eight cakes and set aside to cool (approx. 4 hrs)
- Level, split, fill and assemble each tier (1 hr)

DAY TWO
- Cut and shape each tier (approx. 2 hrs)

- Cover each tier with buttercream (2 hrs including refrigeration)
- Cut holes in the top of the bottom three tiers (½ hr)
- Cover each tier with sugarpaste (1 hr)
- Assemble the tiers (½ hr)
- Decorate each tier (2 hrs)
- Final touches (½ hr)

two (10-cm/4-inch) round vanilla cakes (5 cm/2 inches high)

two (15-cm/6-inch) square vanilla cakes (2 inches (5 cm high)

two (20-cm/8-inch) round vanilla cake (5 cm/2 inches hig

two (30-cm/12-inch) square vanilla cakes (5 cm/2 inches high)

STEP 1

Level the tops of all cakes with the serrated knife. Spread buttercream between each cake pair. Chill the four tiers for 1 hour to firm up the crumb.

STEP 2

Starting with the 15-cm (6-inch) square tier, spread a dab of buttercream on the top of the cake. Place the 10-cm (4-inch) square cake board on top. With the serrated knife, carve around the top edge of the cake, using the 10-cm (4-inch) board as the guide and sloping down to the 15-cm (6-inch) base.

STEP 3

Flip the cake upside down, keeping the 10-cm (4-inch) board on the bottom of the cake. From the 15-cm (6-inch) diameter top, with the serrated knife at a 45-degree angle against the side of the cake, cut straight across to cut a wedge off the top.

STEP 4

Spread some buttercream on the top and put the wedge back on top of the tier, turning it 180 degrees. Cover the entire cake with buttercream and smooth with the dough scraper. Return to the refrigerator for 1 hour.

STEP 5

Repeat steps 2 to 4 with the 30-cm (12-inch) square tier and the 25-cm (10-inch) square board.

STEP 6

Using the 5-cm (2-inch) round board as a guide, trace a 5-cm (2-inch) circle on the 10-cm (4-inch) round board. Cut out the circle with scissors. Attach the circle to the top of the 10-cm (4-inch) round tier with a dab of buttercream. Using the board as a guide, carve around the top edge of the cake and slope down toward the 10-cm (4-inch) base.

STEP 7

Flip the cake upside down, keeping the board attached. Hold the knife at a 45-degree angle against the side of the cake and cut straight across to take a wedge off the top.

STEP 8

Turn the wedge around 180 degrees and attach it to the top of the cake with buttercream. Cover the entire cake with buttercream and smooth with the dough scraper. Chill for 1 hour.

STEP 9

Repeat steps 6 to 8 with the 20-cm (8-inch) round tier and the 15-cm (6-inch) round board.

STEP 10

Using the 15-cm (6-inch) round board as a guide, trace a 15-cm (6-inch) circle in the centre of the top of the 30-cm (12-inch) square tier.

STEP 11

Cut out the circle, down through the entire layer and remove the circle of cake. The 20-cm (8-inch) round tier will sit in this hole. Repeat these steps for the 20-cm (8-inch) round tier with the 10-cm (4-inch) square board and the 15-cm (6-inch) square tier with the 5-cm (2-inch) round board.

STEP 12

Roll out 425 grams (15 ounces) of white sugarpaste to 6 mm (¼ inch) thick and cover the tapered 10-cm (4-inch) round tier. Smooth with the sugarpaste smoother and trim off excess with the pizza cutter, wrapping the trimmings with clingfilm.

STEP 13

Dye 850 grams (30 ounces) of sugarpaste black. Roll out to 6 mm (¼ inch) thick and cover the 15-cm (6-inch) tapered square tier. Smooth with the sugarpaste smoother and trim off excess with the pizza cutter, saving the trimmings for making zebra stripes.

STEP 14

Dye 850 grams (30 ounces) of sugarpaste a light brown. Roll out to 6 mm (¼ inch) thick and cover the 20-cm (8-inch) tapered round tier. Smooth with the smoother and trim off excess. Add trimmings to the remaining sugarpaste.

STEP 15

Dye the remaining sugarpaste a dark brown. Roll out to 6 mm (¼ inch) thick and cover the 30-cm (12-inch) tapered square tier. Smooth with the smoother and trim off excess.

STEP 16

Cut 22 dowels to 9 cm (3½ inches) in length. Insert six dowels vertically into the cut-out hole in the 15-cm (6-inch) tier, eight into the hole in the 20-cm (8-inch) tier and eight into the 30-cm (12-inch) tier. Stack the tiers in decreasing sizes. Sharpen two 30-cm- (12-inch-) long dowels and drive them vertically down through all the tiers, one on either side of the cake.

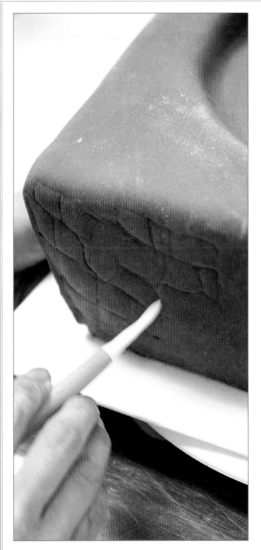

STEP 17

Using the veining tool, gently score the sides of the 30-cm (12-inch) square tier to give an alligator skin effect. Mix brown food colouring with vodka and paint the entire tier. Using the same brown mixture, paint random spots of all shapes and sizes on the 20-cm (8-inch) round tier. Mix black colouring with vodka and add random black outlines to the brown spots to create the look of leopard spots. Paint the entire 15-cm (6-inch) tier with the black food colouring to make it shiny like leather.

STEP 18

Roll out the remaining black sugarpaste to
3 mm (⅛ inch) thick. Use the pizza cutter to cut
out tapered strips. Attach these strips to the
10-cm (4-inch) round tier to create zebra stripes.
Using the leftover black sugarpaste, roll out
¼-teaspoon balls. Arrange these balls along the
base of the 10-cm (4-inch) round tier and the
20-cm (8-inch) round tier.

STEP 19

Fill the piping bag with black royal icing and
pipe dots on the base of the 15-cm (6-inch)
square tier and the 30-cm (12-inch) square tier.

STREET SCENE

This miniature three-tiered cake will transport you to a tranquil street corner around a bakery shop. Let your imagination run wild when adding decorations. The details will amaze your guests. You will need to start one day early for all decorations to dry on time.

TOOLS

- serrated knife
- offset spatula
- 10-cm (4-inch) square cake board
- 13-cm (5-inch) square cake board
- 20-cm (8-inch) square cake board
- dough scraper
- pastry brush
- 30-cm (12-inch) square cake drum
- rolling pin
- pizza cutter
- clingfilm
- sugarpaste smoother
- cobblestone impression mat
- utility knife
- dowels and shears
- pencil sharpener

- ruler and pencil
- parchment paper
- piping bag
- flower former
- wire
- measuring spoons
- square cutters – small and large
- round cutters – small and large
- small sharp knife
- small palette knife
- frill cutter
- oval cutters – small and large
- cocktail sticks
- fine paintbrush
- scissors
- striped ribbon
- glue stick

MATERIALS

- two (10-cm/4-inch) square vanilla cakes (5 cm/ 2 inches high)
- two (13-cm/5-inch) square vanilla cakes (5 cm 2 inches high)
- two (20-cm/8-inch) square vanilla cakes (5 cm 2 inches high)
- 1 kg (2 lb 3 oz) buttercream
- 2.3 kg (5 lb) white sugarpaste
- gel food colouring – black, blue, red, yellow, brown, pink and ivory
- piping gel
- cornflour
- royal icing
- black Candy Melts

OVERVIEW

This cake will require two days to complete.

DAY ONE
- Prepare and make the sugarpaste decorations for each tier (approx. 3 hrs)

DAY TWO
- Make six cakes and set aside to cool (approx. 3 hrs)
- Level, split, fill and assemble the tiers (1½ hrs)

- Cover each tier with buttercream (2½ hrs including refrigeration)
- Cover the tiers with sugarpaste (1½ hrs)
- Cover tiers with cobblestone sugarpaste (1½ hrs)
- Decorate each tier (2½ hrs)
- Assemble all the tiers (1 hr)
- Final touches (½ hr)

two (10-cm/4-inch) square vanilla cakes (5 cm/ 2 inches high)

two (13-cm/5-inch) square vanilla cakes (5 cm 2 inches high)

two (20-cm/8-inch) square vanilla cakes (5 cm/ 2 inches high)

STEP 1

Level the tops of all cakes, split them in half horizontally and fill between the layers with buttercream, working with each tier on its corresponding cake board. Cover tiers with a thin layer of buttercream. Chill until firm. Cover with a second coat of buttercream and smooth with the dough scraper. Refrigerate for 1 hour.

STEP 2

Dye 280 grams (10 ounces) of sugarpaste black, 425 grams (15 ounces) grey, 30 grams (1 ounce) blue, 30 grams (1 ounce) red, 30 grams (1 ounce) yellow, 30 grams (1 ounce) brown, 30 grams (1 ounce) ivory and 30 grams (1 ounce) pink. Leave the remaining sugarpaste white.

STEP 3

With the pastry brush, spread piping gel on the 30-cm (12-inch) cake drum. On a cornflour-covered working surface, roll out the black sugarpaste to 6 mm (¼ inch) thick. Cover the cake drum and trim the excess. Save the trimmings and cover them with clingfilm.

STEP 4

Roll out the white sugarpaste to 6 mm (¼ inch) thick and cover the 20-cm (8-inch) tier. Smooth with the sugarpaste smoother. Trim off excess and save trimmings, covered with clingfilm. Transfer the tier to the prepared cake drum.

STEP 5

Roll out the grey sugarpaste to 6 mm (¼ inch) thick and cover the 13-cm (5-inch) tier. Smooth with the sugarpaste smoother. Trim off excess and save trimmings, covered with clingfilm. Repeat with the 10-cm (4-inch) tier.

STEP 6

Roll out the remaining grey sugarpaste to 6 mm (¼ inch) thick. Place the impression mat on top and roll over the mat with the rolling pin. Lift off the mat, the sugarpaste now has the texture of cobblestones.

STEP 7

Cut out sides with the pizza cutter. Attach with a little water to one side of the 20-cm (8-inch) tier. Trim off excess with the utility knife. Do this until the four sides are covered. Repeat with the 10-cm (4-inch) and 13-cm (5-inch) tiers.

STEP 8

Cut ten 10-cm- (4-inch-) long dowels. Insert six vertically into the 20-cm (8-inch) tier and four into the 13-cm (5-inch) tier. Stack the 13-cm (5-inch) tier on top of the 20-cm (8-inch) tier and the 10-cm (4-inch) tier on top of the 13-cm (5-inch) tier. Sharpen one end of a 30-cm (12-inch) dowel and drive it vertically through the centre of all three tiers.

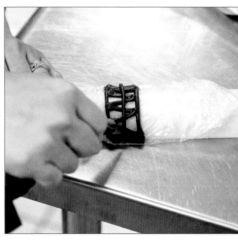

STEP 9

With a ruler and pencil, draw four rectangles, 4 cm (1½ inches) wide and 20 cm (8 inches) long, on a piece of parchment paper. Also make four rectangles, 4 cm (1½ inches) wide and 10 cm (4 inches) long. Dye royal icing black and fill the piping bag. Cut a small hole in a corner of the bag and pipe along the lines on the parchment paper. Pipe circles in the middle of each rectangle and a line through the middle horizontally. These will be the railings, which will go on top of the 10-cm (4-inch) tier and the 20-cm (8-inch) tier. Allow to dry.

STEP 10

To create two balconies, cover a flower former with plastic. Pipe the same design on the flower former as you used to make the railings. Allow to dry.

STEP 11

To make lanterns, cut four pieces of wire 15 cm (6 inches) long. Using the shears, curl one end of the wire into a little hook. Measure out four ½-teaspoon balls of black sugarpaste. Using your fingers, shape the balls into lanterns. Roll out the yellow sugarpaste to 1.5 mm (⅟₁₆ inch) thick and cut out small squares. Attach to the sides of the lanterns and trim off excess with the utility knife. Dip the hooked end of each wire into water and insert into the tops of the lanterns. Set aside to dry overnight.

STEP 12

To make an awning, roll out the red sugarpaste to 1 cm (½ inch) thick. Cut out a large circle with the round cutter. With a knife, cut off a third of the circle from the bottom. Use the palette knife to score lines into the remaining part of the circle (to give texture to the awning). Roll out the white sugarpaste to 1.5 mm (¹⁄₁₆ inch) thick. Using the frill cutter, cut out a scalloped strip. Attach it with a little water to the straight edge of the piece of red sugarpaste.

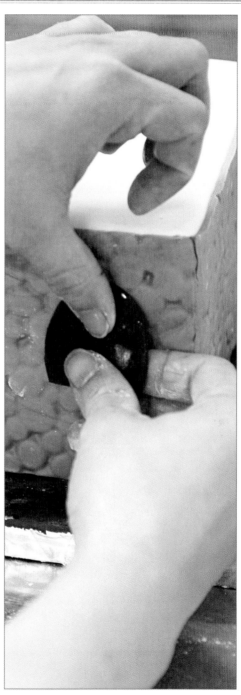

STEP 13

Roll out the remaining black sugarpaste to 1.5 mm (¹⁄₁₆ inch) thick. Using the appropriate cutters, cut out five large ovals and one large square. Also cut out two rectangles measuring 5 cm (2 inches) wide and 10 cm (4 inches) long. With a little water, attach the square to one side of the 20-cm (8-inch) tier. This will be the front door. Cut a third off the bottom of each black oval and attach one on either side of the door to simulate windows. The remaining ovals will be attached to three sides of the second tier. Attach the two rectangles on opposite sides of the 20-cm (8-inch) tier.

STEP 14

Roll out the yellow sugarpaste to 1.5 mm (1/16 inch) thick. Cut out four small ovals, then cut off a third of the bottom of the ovals. Then cut the remaining pieces into four equal parts. Attach these pieces to the black windows to create the look of window tines.

STEP 16

Roll out the blue sugarpaste and cut out a large oval. Cut it in half vertically. Use a small piece of plastic to make the curtain look like it is billowing. Allow to dry overnight. Attach it to the black oval of the front window on the second tier.

STEP 15

With cocktail sticks, attach the red awning to the top of the front door.

STEP 17

Roll out the remaining white sugarpaste to 1.5 mm (1/16 inch) thick. Cut out two rectangles, each 4 cm (1½ inches) wide by 8 cm (3 inches) long. Attach with a little water to the black rectangles. These will be the display windows of your bakery shop. Cut out shapes of cakes from the pink and ivory sugarpaste. Attach to the window with a little water.

STEP 18

Measure out ¼ teaspoon of black sugarpaste. Shape with your fingers into a weathervane. Attach to a cocktail stick and insert it vertically into the centre of the top tier.

STEP 19

Melt a little bit of black Candy Melts in a parchment cone. Carefully remove the railings from the parchment paper. Attach the railings to the top of the 20-cm (8-inch) tier with the melted candy. Carefully remove the balconies from the flower former and attach them to the windows without curtains on the second tier.

STEP 20

Roll out the white sugarpaste to 6 mm
(¼ inch) thick. Cut out four circles. With a
fine paintbrush and black food colouring,
paint on the numbers and hands of the clocks.
Roll out brown sugarpaste to 3 mm (⅛ inch)
thick. Cut out four rectangles measuring 4 cm
(1½ inches) wide and 8 cm (3 inches) long. Cut
out a circle from each rectangle with the circle
cutter used for the clocks. Score each brown
piece with a small palette knife for texture.
These are your shutters. Attach the clocks to
the building. Attach the shutters to the sides of
each clock.

STEP 21

Attach the railings to the top of the 4-inch
(10-cm) tier with some Candy Melts. Insert
the wires of the lanterns into each corner of
the cake drum. Cut the striped ribbon to your
desired size and attach it to the cake drum with
the glue stick.

WEDDING DRESS

In every wedding, the focus is on the bride's dress and the wedding cake.
But what happens when the cake mimics the dress?

TOOLS

- large pastry brush
- 35-cm (14-inch) round cake drum
- rolling pin
- sharp knife
- serrated knife
- offset spatula
- 15-cm (6-inch) round cake board
- two 20-cm (8-inch) round cake boards
- 25-cm (10-inch) round cake board
- dowels and shears
- dough scraper
- sugarpaste smoother
- pizza cutter
- clingfilm
- medium leaf cutter
- piece of thin foam
- round stick
- paintbrush
- sugarpaste ribbon cutter
- pencil sharpener
- ivory satin ribbon
- glue stick

MATERIALS

- piping gel
- 2.8 kg (6¼ lb) white sugarpaste
- cornflour
- two (15-cm/6-inch) round vanilla cakes (5 cm/ 2 inches high)
- one (20-cm/8-inch) round vanilla cake (5 cm/ 2 inches high)
- three (25-cm/10-inch) round vanilla cakes (5 cm/ 2 inches high)
- 1.9 kg (4¼ lb) buttercream
- silver dragées or sugarpaste beads – fine and medium
- pearl dragées or sugarpaste beads – medium
- gumpaste

OVERVIEW

This cake will require two days to complete.

DAY ONE
- Prepare the cake drum and cover with sugarpaste (15 mins)

- Prepare and make the six cakes and set aside to cool (approx. 3 hrs)

- Level, split, fill and assemble each tier (1 hr)

- Cover tiers with buttercream (1½ hrs including refrigeration)

- Cover all tiers with sugarpaste (½ hr)

- Cover the 20-cm (8-inch) tier with silver dragees (10 mins)

DAY TWO
- Prepare the sugarpaste leaves and attach to 25-cm (10-inch) tier (approx. 3 hrs)

- Prepare, make and attach the sugarpaste strips and buttons to the 15-cm (6-inch) tier (2 hrs)

- Insert dowels and assemble the tiers (½ hr)

- Final touches (10 mins)

two (15-cm/6-inch) round vanilla cakes (5 cm/2 inches high)

one (20-cm/8-inch) round vanilla cake (5 cm/2 inches high)

three (25-cm/ 10-inch) round vanilla cakes (5 cm/2 inches high)

STEP 1

With the pastry brush, spread piping gel evenly over the cake drum. On a cornflour-covered surface, roll out 280 grams (10 ounces) of the white sugarpaste to 6 mm (¼ inch) thick and cover the cake drum. Trim the excess with the sharp knife.

STEP 2

Prepare the 15-cm (6-inch) and 20-cm (8-inch) tiers by levelling their tops with the serrated knife, splitting them in half horizontally and filling between the layers with buttercream. Cover with a thin layer of buttercream. Place them on their corresponding cake boards. You will have one 10-cm- (4-inch-) high tier and one 5-cm- (2-inch) high tier.

STEP 3

For the 25-cm (10-inch) tier, level all three cake rounds and split them in half horizontally. Fill between the layers with buttercream. Stack just two of the cake rounds (four layers of cake in total) on the 25-cm (10-inch) board. Cut six pieces of dowel to 8 cm (3 inches) long and insert them vertically into the filled 25-cm (10-inch) cake. Spread a layer of buttercream on top. Place the remaining 20-cm (8-inch) round cake board in the centre. Continue filling with buttercream and stack the remaining 25-cm (10-inch) cake round on top. The result will be a 25-cm (10-inch) tier measuring 15 cm (6 inches) in height.

STEP 4

Cut another six pieces of dowel to 8 cm (3 inches) in length. Insert dowels vertically into the top half of the stacked 25-cm (10-inch) tier.

STEP 5

Spread a thin layer of buttercream on all three tiers. Refrigerate for 20 minutes. Cover the top and sides with a second, thicker coat of buttercream. Smooth with the dough scraper and refrigerate for 1 hour.

STEP 6

Roll out all the remaining white sugarpaste to 6 mm (¼ inch) thick. Cover all three tiers. Smooth with the sugarpaste smoother and trim the excess with the pizza cutter. Save the trimmings, wrapped in clingfilm. Transfer the 25-cm (10-inch) tier to the cake drum, securing in place with a dab of royal icing.

STEP 7

Roll out the leftover sugarpaste to 3 mm (⅛ inch) thick. Using the medium leaf cutter, cut out medium-sized leaves.

STEP 8

One by one, place the leaves on the thin foam and thin the edges with the round stick.

STEP 9

Starting with the base and working your way up, attach the leaves with water to the side of the 25-cm (10-inch) tier until you have covered the entire cake. Leave a 20 cm (8 inch) diameter on the top where the second tier will sit.

STEP 10

Mix 1 teaspoon of gumpaste with 60 ml (2 fl oz) of water to make an edible 'glue'. Brush the side of the 20-cm (8-inch) tier with this glue. Holding the tier at an angle, sprinkle the side with the fine silver dragées or sugarpaste beads. Try to coat the sides as thoroughly as you can. Fill in the gaps without silver dragées with the pearl dragées or sugarpaste beads.

STEP 11

Roll out the remaining white sugarpaste to 3 mm (⅛ inch) thick. With the sugarpaste ribbon cutter, cut 2.5 cm (1 inch) wide strips that are long enough to wrap around the 15-cm (6-inch) tier. Moisten half of the strip lengthwise with water. Fold it over so that the strip is 1 cm (½ inch) wide.

STEP 13

Roll a ½-teaspoon ball of sugarpaste into a button. Attach with a little water to where the ends of the strip overlap.

STEP 14

Repeat until the entire tier is encircled with strips of sugarpaste and you have a row of buttons down the front side.

STEP 12

With the fold side up, attach with a little water to the top of the 15-cm (6-inch) tier. Allow the ends to overlap and trim the excess with a knife.

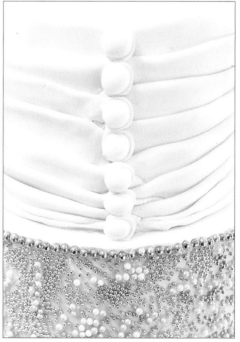

STEP 15

Cut six pieces of dowel, 5 cm (2 inches) long and insert them vertically into the 20-cm (8-inch) tier. Leave a small space of 5 cm (2 inches) from the edge. Place a dab of royal icing on the top of the dowels. Set the 20-cm (8-inch) tier on top of the 25-cm (10-inch) tier. Then, set the 15-cm (6-inch) tier on top of the 20-cm (8-inch) tier. Sharpen a 30-cm- (12-inch-) long dowel. Drive it vertically into the centre of all three tiers. Cover the hole on top with some royal icing.

STEP 16

Using royal icing, attach the medium silver dragées or sugarpaste beads to the top edge and the base of the second tier. Attach the ivory ribbon to the cake drum with the glue stick.

INDEX

A

air bubbles, in sugarpaste 18, 19
airbrushes 11, 45–6, 72
alcohol, food colourings and 8
animal pattern cake 120–7

B

baby shower cake 86–93
baking sheets 11
ball tools 10
bamboo design 30–3
baroque cake 80–5
black & white ribbons cake 34–9
bone tool 102
bows, cutting/forming 48–55,
    90–93, 113–16
brooches, making 114–16
building, designing and making
    128–35
buttercream icing 8
    recipe 14

C

cake boards 10, 20–1
cake drums 10
cake tins 10
cake stands 10
carrot cake 13
chocolate sponge cake 13
circle cutters 27–8, 53, 65,
    88, 131
clay gun 103
clingfilm 11
clothing steamer
    37–8, 105

cobblestone impression mat, 129
colouring sugarpaste 18
colourings 8
cornflour 8
cosmopolitan cake 44–7
cube cake 26–9
cushion design 100–5
cutters, design 11
    blossom 89
    calyx 109
    frill 131
    heart-shaped 44–7, 98
    leaf 137
    letters 44–7
    oval 57, 114
    pastry 27–8, 53, 65, 88, 131
    petals 70
    ribbon 10, 23, 49, 87, 98,
        113, 139
    rose 108–9
    scalloped 93
    square 77
cutters, pizza 10
cutting sugarpaste 19
cutting shapes 45–7

D

damask pattern cake 80–5
decorating
    supplies 8
    techniques 16–21
    tools 10–11
decorations, edible 8
design cutters
    see also cutters 11
design tools 11

dog bone tool 102
dough scrapers 11
dowels, wooden 11, 20–1
dragées 8
drums 10

E

edible decorations 8
edible glitter 8, 71–3, 98, 105,
114–19

F

fancy cushion cake 100–5
feathers, making 115–16
filling cake layers 16–17
five-tier cakes 80–5
flower formers 11
flowers, gumpaste 107–9
food colourings, gel 8
four-tier cakes 62–7
frill cutter 131

G

gel food colourings 8
gift box cake 48–55
glazes 8
glitter, edible 8, 71–3, 98, 105,
114–19
gold leaf, edible 8
guide markings 62–3, 81
gumpaste 8, 138
    flowers 107–11
    feathers 115–16

H
harlequin design cake 94–9
house/shop design 128–35

I
icings 8
    recipes 14–15
impression mats 129
indenting tools 10

J
Japanese-inspired tea cake
    30–3

K
knives 10

L
layers, levelling/splitting/filling
    16–17l
leather-look design 120–7
levelling cake layers 16–17
luster dust 8, 71–73, 98, 105,
    114–19
lustrous peacock cake 112–19

M
marbling sugarpaste 107
Mardi Gras cake 68–75
marking guides 63–4, 81
mask making 69–71
moulding with fingers 128–35

moulds 60, 102
mosaic cake 76–9

N
New York City cake design 44–7

O
offset spatulas 11

P
paintbrushes 11
painter's palettes 11
painting on sugarpaste 33
palette knives 10
parchment paper 11
pastry brushes 11
pastry cutters, using 27–8, 53,
    65, 88, 131
petal dust 8, 31, 73, 81, 82,
    84, 116
petals 70, 108–9
piping bags/tips 11
piping designs 25, 41–3, 73–75,
    114–19, 130–5
piping gel 8
pizza cutters 10
polka dots cake 62–7
preparation techniques 16–17

Q
quilting tool 81, 97

R
recipes
    cakes 12–13
    icings 14–15
ribbon cutters 10, 23, 49, 87, 98,
    113, 139
ribbon roses cake 40–3
ribbon with bow, making 49–55
rolling pins 10
    textured 23
rolling-out sugarpaste 18–19
rose bouquet cake 106–11
roses
    gumpaste 106–11
    sugarpaste fondant 40–3
round cutters 27–8, 53,
    65, 88, 131
royal icing 8, 15
ruffled brooch cake 56–61

S
scalloped cutters 93
scoring tools 10
scrollwork 22–5
separators 112–19
shape cutters see pastry cutters;
shaped cakes 94–9, 100–5,
    120–7
shortening, and drying-out 8
silver leaf, edible 8
spatulas 11
splitting cake layers 16–17
stacking tiers 11, 20–1
    with separators 112–19
stands 10

stencils, using 25, 82–3
store design cake 128–135
street scene cake 128–35
sugar-craft gun 10, 71, 110
sugarpasate, using 8, 18–19
    marbling 107
    moulding with fingers 128–35
    smoothers 10
    tools 10–11
    see also cutters 10

T
textured rolling pins 10. 23
texturing tools 10
three-tier cakes 34–9
tiered cakes, stacking 11, 20–1
    with separators 112–19
tiles, sugarpaste 76–9
tins 10
toothpicks 11
topsy-turvy cake 94–9
turntables 11

U
urban safari cake 120–7
utility knives 10

V
vanilla sponge cake 8, 12
veining tools 10, 102, 125
violet scrolls cake 22–5
vodka, food colourings 8

W
wedding dress cake 136–41
white fat, and drying-out 8
wrinkles, sugarpaste 19

CREDITS

Unless specified, all images are the copyright of Quintet Publishing Ltd, and may not be reproduced without prior written permission. While every effort has been made to credit contributors, Quintet Publishing would like to apologise should there have been any omissions or errors – and would be pleased to make the appropriate correction for future editions of the book.